Liliana De Cristoforo

I0422419

Women Behind Bars

From Alfonsina to Sophia Loren

Titolo | Liliana De Cristoforo

Autore | Women Behind Bars

ISBN | 978-88-31686-78-5

Youcanprint
Via Marco Biagi 6 - 73100 Lecce
www.youcanprint.it
info@youcanprint.it

Introduction

In this book, I tell the experiences acquired during my long job activity, which let me know many women's lives. Very different women, for their age and culture, but joined by their jail experiences, by their sufferance, by the hope in redemption and by the anxiety in recovering their roped dignity.

I had collected witnessed, confidences, confessions dealing with events, which had overwhelmed their lives, leading them to make crimes.

Their lives shifted among ancient problems, as honour killing, prostitution, rope, but also the modern ones, as clandestine immigration, drug addiction, and transsexuality. They are stories of undergone violence, of betrayed love, disillusioned expectations.

Women's tales, victims of men, of society, of prejudices, of bad life circumstances, trapped in complex psychological situations, in which ancient fears, burning frustrations and spirit of revenge found the place.

Inside their souls love gives ground on hate, the hope undergoes to desperation.

Alfonsina is a farmer coming from Irpinia (a place in Campania, in the south of Italy) who, after she had lost her lover in war, was compelled by her family to marry a man, who submitted her to incredible oppressions and humiliations, so that she reacted with crushing consequences. Then Concetta, victim of prejudices and betrayed by her lover. Moreover, Rosa, forever signed by a roping, endured when she was a teenager. Samira, driven by misery, comes in Italy from Nigeria and ends in the hands of a prostitution criminal organization. Elisa did not accept her husband's rules of Mafia, and Teresa, Anna, Olga, and more…

Among them, in 1982 even Sophia Loren was imprisoned for seventeen days in the prison of Caserta, for tax fraud. Her detention had such a big wide appeal, giving raise to paradoxes and grotesque events. However, a part from media gossip and from the curiosity which her arrival gave birth in the other prisoners, she was an out of rich star of the cinema even there, covered by the air of charm and mystery.

Crossing by the protagonists' events, the reader is driven into the discovery of the most hidden sides of a world never completely explored of women's soul. This book is the revisited and expanded edition of Women, gates and crimes. Tales from prison.

ALFONSINA

"Many are surprised by my energy, but do you know how old am I?" The woman, who was talking to me, near the flowerbed she had to take care, showed an old age. Her withered and wrinkled skin, her already grey and thin hair, her almost all teeth lacking mouth, her curved and tired shoulders, witnesses of a painful and troubled life, all led her got the name of "grandma" by her fellows.

To the say the truth, this "grandma" was only fifty-one. She looked at me by her good-natured gentle eyes, almost asking for approval of her job, while I was admiring the beautiful flowers, where spring sunshine exalted their vivid colours. "They are gorgeous", I was compelled to tell her, "and well handled!"

"Do you know?" she said pleased, "I was born surrounded by plants. I had spent my life taking care of animals and farming. You cannot imagine how much dirt I had down. This one is only a joke for me, now."

Alfonsina P. came from a little rural village near Lioni, a lost little agglomerate on Irpinia Mountains, in which people of that time were linked to old life-style and to a basic farming economy. She had three children, adults by now, and many grandchildren. She liked to define herself a farming woman, almost lacking of experiences, except for those dealing with farming and hardship of life. However, difficulties, sacrifices and humiliations she had suffered, never turned up her, as often happens, into a malicious or distrustful woman. Alfonsina had kept her gaiety without malice, as in the past thirty years she showed cleverness and a strong craving for knowledge, always testing new things.

"Love for farming was passed down to me by my father. He was tall, thin, and strong, with black waved hair. He looked like an actor who often appears in movies, that actor…. I don't remember the name…Anyway he looked like an actor." He taught me how to take care of plants and farming, to seed, to fertilize, to trim, to understand the weather changes from wind direction, to foresee the rainfall or dry periods. My father loved me. As a child, when he held me in his arms, I felt sure, safe. I felt nothing could happen to me. I remember he used to take me walking during summertime, through the narrow and steep mountains paths. By his confident and determined step, and by my jumping pace, we used to walk together, until the river. We used to sit on the little wall of the riverbank, admiring the endless never stop- flowing of water. I liked that clear water that uninterrupted movement, that relaxing rustle. Of course, that river is not always calm. Sometimes its strong frenzy and unruly, wild power, threaten to crush everything around, but when I saw it impressive and calm, I could feel joy and peace. My father used to tell me several things: fables, fair tails, legends, old stories about our inhabitants or nearest people; he argued me about human being and world creation, about the birth of things and of existing animals on the earth.

"The river Ofanto, he said, was born from Appennino Mountains, running for many kilometres along Irpinia territories and flowing into Adriatic Sea". "What is sea?" I asked. "It is an enormous expanse of salt water". He answered. I wished I could see the sea, I could not imagine how a huge extended expanse of salt water was. In my life, I have seen only mountains. I have never supposed that one day, inside a prison, I could have seen the sea throughout the window of a jail. My father was

6

loved, estimated by everyone and always ready to help people with their troubles. He was a wise and generous man, deeply devoted to his family. He was an important unique reference point for my mother. If he had lived in this age, he would surely have studied and he would have become a teacher, because of his cleverness and intelligence. His family was wealthy, with some economic trouble after the world war, the first of course. Grandpa handled and nurtured personally his lands. Therefore, he was a farmer, as we say today. After grandpa's death, we inherited a big vineyard and the house where he had lived, in the suburb of the village. It was not big, but in good conditions, with a stall for animals. We were not rich, but we could live in a respectable way. Childhood was the only peaceful period of all my life. My father had never hit me, maybe because I was the only female. He wanted me well behaved and hard working. Moreover, I know he was glad and satisfied of me, because I have always been wise, without flights and fancy in my mind. If he had been with me, my life would surely have been so different.

On the contrary, unfortunately, he passed away. A pneumonia disease brought him away in few days. He had come back from the fields under a violent rainfall; He was soaking wet with cold shivers. He went to bed and he had back up nevermore. I remember the doctor who came at home twice a day. He visited him shaking his head powerless and worried about him. I remember my mother, pale and scared, always next to the bed day and night, as a ghost. I remember the silence, the dark and the gloomy atmosphere, plenty of anxiety. Every day I went to the church, praying for the Holy Virgin Mary. I looked at her motionless, with her light blue mantle and sweet face and I spoke with her, crying, asking…

"Ask and you'll get, knock and you'll be opened" is written inside the Holy Gospel. I had asked, I had knocked many times, but I had always found a locked door. I often listen to something like" God gave me grace!" and sometimes God has nothing to do with it. Anyway, I could never tell it. "God wants to test you" my mother repeated me. "Don't let him down". But why He pretends all those tests to me?" After my father's death, nothing was like before. I had to work hard to manage my family. My brothers were still young and they could do little. I took care of lands; I nurtured animals, keeping on housework. I had no stops and at night, I felt wasted out by hard working and effort. My mother recovered nevermore. I could see her becoming bowed, almost crushed, under the weight of a bitter and heavy existence. She was a fragile and vulnerable creature, to be protected on whom I could not trust. Nevertheless, she, poor woman, she had been just worn out by another terrible loss, happened years before, my brother Vincenzo's death.

He was a nice boy, cheerful, lively, sharp, always going around and playing with his friends. My mother chased him in the streets, to get him back to school. My parents wished him got his primary school education, at least, but he did not like studying at all.

Conversely, I have never been at school, I am illiterate. In my little village, women did not use to study. However, I would have liked to learn reading and writing; I would like to know History, Geography, and Maths. Being ignorant is bad; it's bad when you cannot write a letter, or speak correctly or when you don't understand cultured people speaking. I don't like that. Surely, if my father could, he would let me study, but studying was not a habit in that time. In our little mountain village there is a strange way of thinking. You cannot do what you really want, because of people's rumours. You cannot decide anything without taking into account others' opinion; even your dress or hairdressing can cause rumours. You are not free in that village: everyone knows all of everyone. I understood these things when I firstly came here. At the beginning they seemed to me normal, 'cause I thought everywhere things were the same. Here, listening to my fellows speaking, I have found that, in other places, everyone can do what he wants. Nowadays, even inside the prison, something is changed, you know. Progress has come; TV shows us what is happening in the world, emigrants had come back home and brought news, Youngers go studying abroad, and today they can do what yesterday they could not.

One day Vincenzino got ill. He had high temperature; the doctor thought about a flu, whereas it was tetanus. Vincenzino had injured himself by a plow, while he was playing. He said nothing, worried about a punishment. He put a bandage on the wound made by rags and hid it under the cloths. It was late when my mother realized it and nothing could be done. He was only seven. He was my elder brother. I remember the little white coffin, covered on by flowers at the base of the altar, my mother and my father's despair, all citizens' sorrow, the silent and distressed funeral procession. Since then, my mother had been dressed in black being in mourning, and she had given it back nevermore.

When my father had reached Vincenzino in the same grave, I used to go often the cemetery, leaving flowers I collected in the fields. I was used to speak to my father, telling him about troubles at home, my worries. It was a way to feel him alive and next to me, since I had nobody to let in on. It seemed to me he could still listen to and help me.

9

A summer mourning, when I was fifteen, while I was going out of the cemetery, thinking about my thoughts, someone suddenly barred my way on, holding my arm. It was Raffaele Salieri, a young man I had always hated, since my childhood, because of his cruelty and insolence. Something in his ambivalent, deceptive glance disgusted me; that's why I had always avoided him. My repulsion got him angry, and when he met me, he looked at me hostile and mocking. That day he strongly caught my arm as in an iron grips and he dragged me on, towards the cemetery keeper's empty hovel, without saying a word. The street was desert and silent; at that hour everyone was working in the fields or was busy in their things. Only the creaking of the gravel under our shoes could be heard, in addition to my scared and painful grooms. Fear paralyzed me. I did not completely understand what he wanted; I was only an ingenue girl, but I found the strength to react using the other arm, punching him. I could hear his heavy breath and see his sweaty getting wet his forehead, trying to win my endurance. He had almost managed to get me into the hovel when I could hear the noise of clatter hooves, maybe a donkey or a mule, and somebody's voice who was riding it, spurring it to go faster. By all the breath I had, I could give a high-pitched scream, which had surprised Raffaele. Taking advantage of his temporary uncertainty, I kicked his leg. I saw him bending over, feeling his slackening off my arm. By a violent jerk, I could get and run out. I run as a damned along the street, even if I realized He wasn't following me. I got home in a panic, breathless, with my heart in my throat, but I did not tell anything to anyone. That fact upset me. The days later, thinking back on it, I shivered frightened and for the avoided danger. I had lost my bravery in going out alone and I prayed God not to meet him anymore on my path. Maybe He was interested on me and he was angry for my repulsion. I was not ugly, do you know? Of course, I am old now and in bad way, but I was not so bad. I was little, but I had straight legs, delicate features, curly long hair as my grandma Alfonsina, my father's mother, who gave me her name, as it was used in my village.

She was a special woman clever and learned: she knew how to count and maybe she could read. Not just because she went to school, of course, but also because she had a great deal of initiative. She managed her own general store, the only one in Lioni. One of those shops in which you can find everything: the farming tools, cookware, cloths, cough drops. In other words everything, even toys. When I was a child, she sometimes gave me one of the toys she sold. They were very simple: a rag doll, a toy wood train, a Jump rope, but they seemed to me precious and luxury gifts. My grandma knew a lot of things. She had travelled a lot. She had been in places around, as Avellino and even in Naples. She told me the buildings in the cities were big and high, with many floors and there were very large and crowded streets, were coaches, cars and other means of transports on railways, called cable cars went around. I would have liked to visit Naples. Life is so strange! I had seen Naples when I first came into prison, just me that I had never moved from Lioni. I had seen very little of it, of course, only what I could have seen from the windows of the police car, when they brought me here and when they escorted me to the Assize Court for the trial, but it was enough for me. What a chaos, a confusion, what a difference with my little and calm village. Well, who Knows if my little village is really so calm or instead, if it hides a secret hell into deep.

As the time passed, my mother became more and more listless. Little and thin, in her black faded dress, whit her suffering expression and her eyes, consumed by tears, she spent her days praying in front of my Dad and Vincenzino's pics. Nothing changed for me. I had been still farming, housekeeping and feeding animals. My brothers started helping me, by their growing up. At the age of seventeen, I became a little woman who had no sureness of the future. At the village, families often organized weddings and my father's death had prevented any plan on me. I could see my peers already engaged, who were going to get married and I felt sad for my future, which had no encouraging expectations. It was just in that period that I felt in love with Andrea, Margherita's son, my godmother.

Godparent's ties were a sort of kinsfolk. Godparents are people to be respected, to whom you have to give presents at Christmas and you have to invite to families parties. Mrs Margherita was a farmer, too. She helped her husband Ettore, taking care of her family with great dignity. Everyone in my village knew and appreciated her kindness and goodness. Andrea was very similar. He was 4 year older than I was. He was handsome and nice, always smiling, kind and gentle with everyone. He had large shoulders, straight back, blonde eyes and hair. Yes, even his eyes were blonde, golden, just like the stone with which some necklace are made; …amber, yes his eyes were amber colour. We had been friends since childhood, and we often met when our families met, but I had never seen him by loved eyes. One evening after a working day, tired and gloomy for my useless and hard life, I looked out of my kitchen window in the street. It was October and the air was getting cooler. Winter starts soon in my country, and it is very freezing, but the sky was clear and full of stars, with a brighten Moon, shining on roofs, streets and fields. Andrea was coming back from the country after the grape harvest. He was walking slowly and weary. When he arrived under the window he saw me, he smiled me and said: "What are you doing? ". "I am looking at stars," I answered with a voice broken by the emotion. He had a moment of hesitation, as he was thinking about something else, while he was looking at me. Then, he said: "Will you come to the grape party next Sunday?" In the meanwhile, his father, his brothers and workers with honkeys and coaches reached him, coming back from vineyard. I had only the time to nod. Then He went away with the others. I saw him moving away through the narrow streets and disappeared over the houses. My heart beat strong, I felt growing inside my soul a strong feeling which made me happy. A sudden feeling for a person I had always known. I went to sleep fantasying.

That night I made a dream, which I could explain only after many years. My father was walking along the solitary street, with a gloomy expression in his face, keeping two wicker wine bottles in his hands. All at once he stopped. He took from his pocket a glass and poured the liquid of one of them inside it and he offered me the glass as to taste it. It was a generous and red ruby wine, of a strong flavour. While I was drinking it, a big black dog appeared, as it wanted to attack us. The opened wicker wine bottle fell down, breaking and spreading all the wine on the floor. I drank the other wine, from the other wicker, but this time was a turbid, black liquid, sour and bitter, disgusting and sickening. The following days, that dream came always back into my mind. I went to an old wise clairvoyant of the village. She foresaw the further two grape crops: one good and the other insufficient and poor quality. To say the truth, the dream had anything but another meaning. The grape harvest was an important and merry event in my village. You could see coaches and beasts of burden moving slowly under the weight of 100lb, leading from the vineyards to the crushing places and women, going through the paths of the country, with huge hang in balance baskets on their head, full of smelling and ripe grape bunches. A joyful atmosphere was everywhere. You could hear voices and songs resounding all over the wide valley, melting with the river gurgling. Whole families, from grandparents to grandsons were busy into the grape harvest, with joyful diligence. Adults and children, by naked foot and dirty cloths, were crushing grape inside huge wooden vats or in ancient millstones. In any place, the smell of fermenting must spread out. It was a testing moment of one's own year job results for everyone.

Last Sunday of October, there was a big party in the square of the village. Some keen women used to cook pancakes, sausages and slide ham and cheese. Then it was used to eat, sing, dance until late in the night, with the music of squeezeboxes, which many could play. It was a simple party and one of the few chance to make meetings and to have fun. That Sunday I dressed with accuracy, I put on my only decent suit I had, that for important events, I put on my earrings received by my grandma and combed my hair for long, left untied on the back. At the party, I sang and danced all night long with Andrea. We looked into each other eyes, laughing with joy. I could see him again in his black suit and white shirt, his face, made red by the wine and the exiting dancing, the easy step and his usual joyful smile. I had only a bad memory of all that day: the angry and frightful glance of Raffaele, which fixed me all the time trough out the crow. That night I didn't sleep, spending many hours to daydream, holding my pillow. I felt this feeling growing wildly, filling up my heart with joy. Few days later Andrea waited for me out of my home path and gifted me with a little bunch of fields' flowers. I had always loved flowers; their colours and their smell give joy to the spirit. With his red face and trembling legs for the emotion, I came back home, keeping those flowers tight to my breast, firmly but gently, trying not to waste them, as I was holding a treasure. That gesture was his declaration of love. Speaking was embarrassing for lovers at that time, a glance or a smile were enough to show their feelings. Hereafter, we often met after work. Stones on the edge of the street were our makeshift chairs. We spoke a lot about us, about our families, about our dreams. At last, there was somebody to speak about my problems, who could listen to me, giving advice or simply support me. His manners reminded my father and his words, giving a deep sense of peace. I felt confident and happy. Before leaving for the war, Andrea came home, giving me a little golden ring with a little red stone and spoke with my mother and my uncle Domenico, my father's brother. "When the war will be ended," he said, "If God lets me come back, I will marry Alfonsina. I am a poor farmer, but I m a good willing worker. We will manage to live with dignity, by our love and regard which link each other, growing up a big and beautiful family, just as I like." I put the box with the little ring inside a drawer of dresser and sometimes I put and turned it among my fingers, waiting, hoping and daydreaming our future. We would have had many children, male and female, a little and modest, which I would have kept always cleaned and tidy. I dreamed about the wedding day, the guests, the ceremony and the banquet. I would have worn my mother's wedding dress with my mother in law's veil, because she had never had daughters.

I went on to live my life as usual, with my heart full of hope and wait I was preparing my hope chest, working and praying, praying a lot. I went to the church, I kneeled in front of the holy Mary and I stayed there, silently, trying to find an inmost and spiritual way to communicate. To say the truth I felt the Holy Mary wouldn't hear anything and anybody, but I believed, I wanted to believed; I realized that, losing my faith I would lose the my only one support. My soul was trustful because I thought God had just deprived me a lot, so that he could not take me Andrea off, too. I do not know why I was convinced of that idea; maybe it was only the denial to look inside the truth. Only now I understand that life never make a balance between "give and take" but it takes, and gives, by chance. There are no rules: it gives a lot to somebody and conversely nothing or few to other. For affection and respect, I often went to Mrs Margherita. I gave her eggs and cheese and I stayed there speaking with her for long. Together we felt both near to Andrea. We tried to know something about war, waiting with anxiety to know news from the radio during the night or we hoped to receive letters but nothing arrived. The echoes from the war in the village were just barely perceived, the rumbling of airplanes and fighter-bombers flying on skies and mountains. Sometimes, at night, far flash on horizon line made think about bombings on cities and on big areas of Irpinia. After many months, a letter from Andrea arrived. Uncle Domenico read it. It was a great moment. A long letter written with uncertainty, to let us know he was in Piemonte, at the boundary of France, that he was homesick and he always thought about me. War was cruel but he met many soldiers coming from other parts of Italy. After that nothing more, no news for long.

Other months had passed. One evening I was coming back, it was April, the valley was green, full of lush plants, faraway I could see the Ofanto, the river were I used to walk with my father. I could see the clear and shining water inside the pink light of the sunset and I imagined the sweet rustling flowing. War made everything very sad; many Youngers of the village had left, many families were in anxiety, many arms lacked for farming. I set down for a while on a big stone and I Thought of my father, to his smile and to the confidence he gave me, the certainty he made me fell. Everything vanished in a while. His memory caused me a stabbing pain to my heart. I thought about Andrea, about I knew nothing about him. My future, clear and planned until little time before, became more and more insecure and foggy. I took my path again with a great sense of anguish inside my soul.

Not far from my home I saw a group of women talking silently with my mother, sit on the stairs, in her shabby black dress and her painful expression in her face. As soon as she noticed me, she had a little tremble, putting down her look and she said: "Unfortunately I have to give a bad news".

So, dreams and illusions vanished, a pillar of my life fell down, and that collapse would have made completely crumbled all my existence. I did not know how I spent those days I do not remember. An absolute sense of useless and emptiness had the run of my life. At the age of nineteen, I felt finished. However, life went on. The war ended, many youngers came back home and among these Raffaele, too, who had never forgot the habit

17

of looking at me in a smug and (annoying) irritating way. I knew I made a sin, I knew I would had never thought about it, but I often thought: why was he alive, instead of Andrea? Respectful of Andrea's memory and of my sorrow, I decided I would have never married anymore. I put my trousseau in a chest, thinking about to give it to one of my niece and I tried to live in the memory of that love I had had no time to grow up. I had no grave on which I could cry and this was another sufferance for me, which I strongly believed in the cult of deaths. I put Andrea's pic on chest of drawers and I made it sure that fresh flowers were always in front of his pic. The little ring with the red stone remained in its box forever.

A Sunday, coming back from Church, I found my uncle Domenico in the kitchen arguing with my mother. I had just come in when He said: "There is a younger who wants to marry you. Yesterday his father came and told me that." A baleful auspice flooded inside of me. "I won't marry anyone" I firmly cut off. "You Have to marry", he replied despotically. "There is no reason to give it up. Andrea was not your husband and now he is death, by no one's guilty. You are so lucky somebody wants you after your engagement. Moreover, a refusal without reason would mean an insult for that family. They are good people and the son Raffaele is maybe an idle boy, but all in all he is a basic boy without hard requires. What would people say if you denied a wedding without a real reason?" one more time people's judgment was the central problem. I believe that in little villages like mine, beyond the need to do what others expected, there is a hidden fear not to be accepted or to be kept out by community. "I won't marry". I desperately repeated. "You must settle down". He answered again. After my father's death, my uncle had the authority of a family leader and he had decided over me. My will did not matter at all, nor my peace of mind. "My father would have never forced me such a thing!" I said crying. I would have liked to rebel, cry, break everything, run away, instead I made nothing and I married Raffaele.

The wedding day I cried all the time. "The bride gets emotional, many said. I do not know if they really believed it or it was a way to cover my feelings, with pity. We went to live far from that village, in open country, in a house, a real shanty, which he inherited from a death uncle, who did not consider the idea to refurbish or paint. A wooden stagger stair, a grimy and smoky kitchen, two dark rooms with a beamed roof, run down floor, and everywhere there was a light spreading humid smell of mould. In the little courtyard there was a water well, an outdoor toilet, and a stable. It was a burning hot house during summertime and icy in winter because of unhinged windows and thin walls. The light came from oil lamps. I had been there for thirty years. The electric light and domestic water settlements came after ten years. My hell began immediately, right away. My husband had no lands, nor job. My mother game us a little piece of land and two cows, which let us barely live. Everything was on my shoulders, the house, the fields and animals. I had to wash cloths at the public washhouse and I was also forced to chop the wood for the chimney. I got up at sunrise and at night, I was destroyed for the strain. He used to spend his mornings sleeping and the evenings at the inn drinking and playing cards or bocce. When he came home late in the evening, he was always drunk and venting his inmost violent instincts, he used to find every false pretence to hit me with punches, kicks, even with sticks or belts. Many times, I was compelled to find shelter in the stable, spending all the night long paralyzed by cold and fear. One night, it was very late, and I was already in the bed; He came home with a woman in a low-necked dress, with lipstick and nail polish. I had never seen her. She looked like a foreigner. He put me off the bed, saying: "go away, the bed will be for us this night!" I had an instinctive reaction. I rebelled and cried. Had he arrived until this point? No respect for his wife and his family dignity? It was an outrageous shame! Then, he took a spade, which was there at hand among the other farming tools and hit me many times, until I fainted. I woke up many hours later, I do not know exactly how many. I felt terrible sticks on my head and I could not open my eyes, nor make a movement. I realized He tied me with a rope, in the stable, near the ring for the animals. I had my eyes swollen, my clothes were bloody soiled, wounds and bruising everywhere. I remained seized up in that condition for long, anguished by pain and thirsty, dived in the crap. I tried to cry, but I was forceless. In that desert area, it was difficult that somebody could hear me. It was late in the morning when he came and untied me. I waited he went to the inn as usual and with few energy I ran to my mother. She took me for few days, giving treatments to my wounds, helping me to get well, but then he forced me to come back home. "A wife must stay with her husband, whatever it happens". She said. " You cannot leave him, it would be a shame. There was a great anxiety inside the family. Uncle Domenico and my father in law chimed in discussion, talked to me and to Raffaele, admonished him, warning him not to repeat it again. They made him to promise something he would have never honoured and so I came back home.

Few time later I realized I was waiting for a baby. I was happy. At least, I would have somebody to love and I would have been loved, too. I would have had a reason of life. I thought ever for Raffaele everything would have been different, he would have the daring to mistreat me anymore. He would have had to respect his son and me. Alas, how many vanishing expectations! I had spent years under many troubles, encouraged only for my children's love, who, nothing could do against their father, dull and violent even with them. I had talked to the priest, to my relatives: everyone told me to bear and pray. If someone tried to chime in, trying to make him reason out, things went better. It had been a long and slow ordeal. I underwent everything: abuses, bushes, moral and physical violence, humiliation, chagrin. I do not know how I had survived. After my mother's death, my brothers sold the few properties and went to America. Uncle Domenico, who had inherited my grandma's shop, got off the business and moved to Avellino. My family vanished.

In that way, years had passed in that house, more and older and tumbled down. My son had soon settled down. The females had married very young, and the son had found work in the north. I remained completely alone. I hoped he got clam with the aging, but it did not happen. Even if for a period, he was calm, so that it seemed to have changed his character; his own choleric and rude spirit came always out. During last times, I took shelter to my married daughter who lived in the same village, but he always came and brought me back home, more and more enraged, more than ever. Two year ago, after one of the last slams suffered, I had been in the hospital for many broken bones. It had not been the first time. I told I had fallen on the stairs, or to have injured myself while farming. I was ashamed. About what? I do not know. When my daughter brought me back home, he was not in. I set down in front of the chimney, extinguished. I was weak and tired. Many times, I had thought to that dream and now I had interpreted it. The wine with sweet taste represented Andrea; the sour and bitter one represented the man I would marry. By this time, I knew, soon or later, the poison of that wine would have killed me.

Next morning I got up very early, It was still night, an icy snap invaded the room. He was sleeping; I could hear him strongly snoring. I could sniff a strong smell of alcohol from his breath. I wanted to light on the chimney but there was no wood. I put on my cloths to get it out in the woodshed. I went towards the door, down to the stairs and I went in the warehouse. It was very dark and it took few minutes until I got my bearing. I got next the wall where the axe was normally placed. All at once, I touched it. I got it. A horrible thought flashed into my mind. I came back, got up to the stairs and went silently next the bed. He was still snoring, laying down with his open mouth, giving out those sharping and irregular whistles. I could not stand those whistles anymore, that animal rasping breath, that smell of wine, that lazy body, that shabby man. I hated him, as I hated that hostile bad, that dark house, that smell of mould, that stupid resignation of mine. I could not see anything, only the shadow of a useless existence. A compulsive anger made me contract my innards and it crossed all over my body until it blew my stack. I gathered my all the strength I had, I rose the axe and hit him many times. He had no time to react. I think he did not realize anything. When I saw all that blood spraying everywhere and his head rolling over my feet, I realized what I had done. If I had not killed him, sooner or later, he would have killed me. It had been all so unreasonable, but could I stand it forever? What Could I do? Where I could go? I am a poor illiterate, sole farmer; nobody has ever taken care of me. Now I am looking for that calmness I had never had to stay with my children and my grandchildren.

Do you know? When I was thinking about the prison. I imagined it as a place where you suffer hunger and thirst pans, with dark, humid and dirty prison cells, full of mice and beetles. Whereas here, you can eat three times a day, the rooms have toilets, heating and from the windows, you can also look at the sea. I did not know the prison in this way. There is a paid job, the garden, the school and even the hairdresser. It does not seem to me a prison, the jail, the true one, the one I had been living for thirty years, and it was at home. To say the truth, if I had known what the prison really was, I would have killed my husband before".

The Granma' was condemned to eleven years of prison; the penalty has been reduced to seven years after the Court of Appeal sentence. She went out in April 1980. Her conquered serenity lasted only seven months. She died under the ruins of her collapsed house during that terrible earthquake in November 23, which upset Italy, destroyed Irpinia and her whole village.

Pozzuoli, 1975.

CONCETTA

Concetta was thirty-five, high and thin, always sad in her face, on which little wrinkles have signed too early. She was a responsible leader cooker, with great sense of duty. She used to prepare carefully the fixed menu, measuring out the quantities established by the ministry and in particular, she took care of the pots and pans, of carts and of the cooktop cleaning. She had a great influence on her friends, maybe for her educational level, even if it was not so high, but it let her emerge from a crowd of people whose cultural level was very low, or maybe because of her serious and responsible attitude, which gave her respectability and reliability.

She came from Sessa Aurunca, an ancient agricultural little city of historical value, in the district of Caserta. She had been standing in prison for fifteen years and she was waiting for the conditional freedom with great anxiety and worry, aware she had plentifully paid her debt with society. Sitting in my office, on the other side of my writing desk, she stared at the window, with her sorrowful eyes and her regretful gaze.

"As a child I was lively, sure not as my brother Costantino, who was terrible. I did not like female toys: bungee cord or dolls annoyed me. I preferred shooting with water gun, rolling on the grass or running in the streets, shouting and laughing in my dirty cloths and my muggy hands, as Costantino did. No, conversely I could not. I was female, and as a female, I had to behave, holding myself back to play with other girls in courtyard in my clean dress and white socks. No tomboyish plays for me. "The boys must behave as boys, and girls must behave as girls", my mother often

24

said, and even if I was little, I perfectly understood what was the meaning of that statement.

However, even if I understood that meaning, I had never accepted it. I had always hated these differences, which I have ever seen as a discrimination. It was clear that Costantino, as all the other boys, was a privileged, although he was less myrmidon and more naughty than I was. Just for this, when I could, I played unseen by soldiers, marbles, even if I felt guilty a little bit later, as if I had made a crime. Growing up, I went to school and I forgot tomboyish plays. However, I felt a deep sense of injustice when I saw my brother could manage his life freely, whereas I had many duties and limits. I had to help my mother in housekeeping, I could go out only during holidays or Sundays, I was not allowed to put on my make-up, nor put on showy or tight dresses. I could only have friends gone down the well with my parents. It is useless to list more.

To sum up, I suffered an education, which led woman to undergo to strict rules, confining her to a subjected role. That was the significant culture in those times in the place where I lived, an old-fashioned view of life, law- abiding and faithful to traditions and a strong sense of honour. Now I can realize how I unconsciously was infected by that manner I strongly disagreed. We cannot live for long in a place without absorbing its habits. It had happened to me. The country influenced me. Without awareness, I finished to behave as my fellow citizens. Thinking over what had happened to me, I realized how much that kind of education had influenced my personality. Now I have changed a lot. My experience taught me to think on my own, and not on prejudices. I understand that if you want to get free from injustice you need to rebel against it. I often see on TV and read on newspaper about women groups in Italy, France and in England in squares or in the streets, waving symbols and shouting slogans, claiming for women freedom from millenary culture, made up of abuse of power and injustice. If I was in another place and I lived in Rome, or in Paris I would parade, me too.

At school, I easily learnt. I liked studying very much and marks were good. After my compulsory graduation, I told my parents I wanted to continue my studies and I was going to attend the high school for teachers. My father was contrary. He did not agree the fact I could stay in mixed classes with boys and girls or I would have to travel every morning to get school. In short, he was worried because I could escape from his control, and you know: "women must stay at home, marry and make children!" that was his belief, and he was not the only one. Women who could study were few. Getting the compulsory graduation was already enough as a target.

It was just then that my mother lost her prejudices and her axioms and firmly sided me up. Although she had a little education, she strongly wished to improve and get her children to emerge. Her cousin was a teacher, who, for short, had been mayor in a little village around us and he was respected in and out family. The idea that I could match uncle Giovanni's achievements swelled her with pride and she did not want to give up this satisfaction, considering she did not expect good results from her son.

Facing with that women's determination, my father was defeated. In his own way, he was a good man. Wine was his passion, not because he was a drunker, but because he was oenologist- winemaker. He spent many times taking care of several and large vineyards, estate which the family inherited from generation to generation. In autumn, the grape harvest was a real ritual, but the various phases of production were the most important things. From the crushing of the grape, the fermentation of must to the bottling. I remember the huge barrels in the cellars, filled of must and the several bottles, carefully stored in the dark, inside which the wine had been saved for years. My father used to taste it, to look carefully out the colour, the clearness of the liquid and used to state the success of the year.

When I got my graduation, my parents gave a great party. Many friends and relatives came to, among them even uncle Giovanni. My mother laid on a big table in the garden, with embroidered tablecloths and porcelain dishes. She prepared a fantastic buffet: lasagne, cannelloni and pizzas of various kind, wild game, and vegetables cooked in several ways, everything watered by special wine of course, coming from my father's wine cellars and at the end, many desserts with sparkling wine to drink to. My mother was glowing and my father happy and pleased. My parents' satisfaction was a source of pride for me: that certification gave me a leading position in my family that I had never had before. I promised I would have never disappointed the expectation of whom believed me, and above all, of myself.

At that point, my parents would have liked me engaged with someone, to marry as soon as possible someone among the several suitors, who were getting to step forward. Among these, there was one considered a good catch, not to leave out, but I did not like him at all. He was a little boorish and I was only nineteen and I did not think to the wedding yet. "Now you have to find a good boy, of a good family, and you have to get married," my mother said. "Youth flies away very soon and I want to see you settled down. You have to give me many grandchildren. I will help you to grow them up". I decided to take my time. "I have to make up my mind, mum, because I would give my public examination to become a teacher, before. After the marriage, I would have no more time." I started to teach in a private school of nuns. The wage was low, but in that way, I could get score for the inclusion inside the list of candidates to teach in public school. That first job was a wonderful experience; I found how great my love for children was. They were so tender when they repeated the alphabet with their little voices. I devoted to them with care and I knew how to treat them. Their progresses were a stimulus for me for doing more and better. I put in to practice what I had learnt: the global method, useful to get learning fast results and the most important didactic methods of great thinkers, as Rousseau, Gentile, Montessori. I was strongly motivated by the nuns' appreciation and by students' parents. The first months of school flow away.

Christmas holidays came soon. At Eve night, I was with my friend Adele inside the cathedral to celebrate the midnight Mass. There were many people, coming from the nearest villages, so many that there was no place to sit. During the Bishop's sermon, I felt as someone was watching me. Turning myself back, I saw a young boy in the opposite side aisle who was smiling at me. I did not know who he was. I had never seen him. That smile upset me, getting embarrassed. I met him at a friend's party on New Year day. I liked him at once; he was friendly, with a deep glance and charming smile, which seduced me. He was a surveyor in a business building company, working for a new highway linking a big centre around.

His name was Armando and he was thirty-one. I realized he was interested at me and I felt pleased. We spent all the night talking. To say the truth, he had been speaking all the time. He told me about his job, his expectations, and his plans for his career. He described his city, Capua and his family: his father was a shopkeeper, his mother a housewife, and spoke about his two sisters. He always had a topic for conversation and I was listening to him kidnapped. His way of speaking seduced me, he had a deep voice and a linguistic fluency, which few people had. I would have been listening to him for hours. I fell in love at once, of a total and unconditional love. A period of daydreams and anxiety started for me.

It was a right manner that a boy, with serious intent for a girl, would talk with her parents immediately, to get the opportunity to meet her. It was also used the habit that the lovers would have never been left alone. They always had to be followed and observed by a relative, both indoor and outdoor. Obviously, it was a real agony for two lovers who wish to stay together. Therefore, we decided to push back our public engagement to meet freely. Anyway, it was difficult to meet, because I seldom could go out alone, without rising doubts.

Moreover, in the village there are always thousands of eyes, watching you wherever you go. I started to come up with travelling to Caserta, to ask for information about the list of teachers, about programs for the public examination and for the dates of the final exams or similar, at the board of education office. I took the bus early in the morning in Sessa and I arrived in Caserta where Armando was waiting for me. He had recently bought a car, a little runabout, which became our shelter. We went around, in the countries, in the woods, in places set apart, where we could stay

29

alone, talk and hug for hours; than in the afternoon, I took the bus back to Sessa. He had the ability to manipulate my will and I could not stand! He managed to make me do what he wanted, convincing me it was my own choice. He was the target of my thoughts and plans; he became the focus of my life. When I could not see him, pretending to study, I spent my time closed in my room writing him love letter, which I gave him as soon as I met him. Armando came in touch with Adele's brother, and that gave us the chance to meet at their house, occasionally in appearance.

Adele has been my friend for all my life. As children, we used to play together and, growing up, we still have been friends, telling our secrets and supporting each other. She has been always by my side, in each moment of my life, sad and happy. I had not seen her since I came here, but we normally write to each other. Even if she is married and she has three children now, she always finds time to think about me, to write letters and send me books. She did not like Armando very much, something of him did not convince her, but she did not understand exactly what. Nevertheless, she supported me. Anyway, I spent few time with him. We put a two days pilgrimage in Rome to good use. It was organized by the church of the village to meet the Pope and to visit the city. With Adele's complicity, I could go away from the rest of the group and meet him, who came alone. Those two days in Rome were wonderful: the last hours of happiness, before the tempest shocked my life. We went around the city: Piazza di Spagna, Colosseo, Fontana di Trevi, via Condotti. We used to eat in little country "trattorie" or in hash houses and, in the evening, we used to walk along the river Tevere. We had no doubt, in those moments, about what would be our love result, or about my future with him. In these years spent inside this prison, I have often thought about that period, about how could it happen to me all that? A daydream, it seems like it never happened to me, but to another one. I realized my father was right when he spoke about women weakness: Had I been weak? Unwary? After all, I was only twenty and I had no experience. I put love above everything, above traditions, conventions, honour. After the trip in Rome, life went on as usual. My mother became annoying, suspecting something: "People in the village say you have a soft spot for the surveyor of the business building company, haven't you? Why don't you let the family meet him? Your father knows nothing yet about, but soon someone will tell him it, you know, and you also know he will get very angry. Try to avoid it."

One day in the morning, while I was in the classroom, I felt a strong sense of nausea, together with strong dizziness. For I while I felt lost, with my head in my hands. It was in that very moment I realized my strange feelings during the last period, and the unusual reaction of my body to some smell and taste. I realized to be pregnant. I managed to meet Armando and to talk about it. He told me not to be worried, everything would be ok, he would meet my parents and we would marry. "I will let my family know about it. You have to wait only ten days. They have gone to Torino to my mother's brother, who is very ill. As soon they come back, I will talk with them and then I will come to your house. Take it easy!"

After few days spent in great anxiety, I noticed, terrified, that I was getting fat more and more. I barely could wear my cloths, which became more and more tight fitting. I went around my house in a grip of anxiety. I woke up in the middle of the night, suddenly scared and upset by nightmares. At school, I was ineffective, jumpy, absent minded. I fixed the children absently, without hearing them, having lost my ability to concentrate. I could not wait for the end of the lessons, because I could not afford the psychological stress I was forced to. My job, the job I had always made with diligence before, became soon an agony. Fortunately, the end of the school year was going to an end and I was waiting it as a relief. Inside my family they understood that something went wrong; my mother became nagging, my father reserved and suspicious.

Ten days had passed, and so other ten. Armando was not seen anymore. I was told that the work for the highway were almost finished and he was sent to another building site. He was completely vanished. I was afraid that something had happened to him, but inside of me, terrible doubts started to come out. The only thing I could do was finding him out in his city. Adele's brother gave me his address, known thanks to a worker of the company: via 4 Novembre, n°68.

Adele and I went to Capua by bus. We easily found the street, which was quite central. The civic numbers were confused and provisional. So, we asked to a shoemaker who was working outside his door. He pointed at the building on the opposite side of the street. We went closer it. From the front door, a young woman with a baby in her arms was coming out. "Do the Family Coletta live here?" we asked. "We are looking for a surveyor whose name is Armando Coletta." "My husband is not in. He is in Naples now for work. He will be back in the afternoon." I folded up as I had received a shot in my stomach. Adele kept my arm and dragged me away. The woman did not notice my reaction, the pale on my face, because she was busy with her baby, who was making fit. "Who is looking for him?"

she said, but we bluffed into not listening to her and we went away quickly.

I could see a huge hurricane falling on my life, which soon would overwhelm me. I could imagine the wind of scandal blowing in each street of the village, the gossip spreading from mouth to mouth, the blame of nuns, of the priest, of the sanctimonious people who used to spend their evenings making gossip, the gaze of disregard of many. An unmarried mother in that period, in a village like mine, was unacceptable. A love child was considered a shame and a relationship with a married man was a heavy fault. Law had not contemplated the divorce, yet and I could not see any future in advance for me. I thought even to an abortion, but who could help me? The abortion was a crime. It would be difficult to find a helpful doctor. I had listened to some midwives who made illegal abortion, but it was very unsafe and very expensive too. I had not so much money. Moreover, killing a baby scared me. I could not understand which was the lesser of two evils, if I had to get rid of him, or let him be born.

Days passed and I could not find any solution to my problem. I could have killed myself and so, put an end to each problem or I should have confessed to my parents everything, facing with their reaction, but I was not so brave. I was struggling among many thoughts inside, as much as that little being was growing up inside my belly, who consciously I refused and unconsciously I wished.

Here came the celebration of the Patron Saint. The whole village was under holiday, with lights, stands, marching band and merry –go – rounds for children. In the years before, I have waited with anxiety that event, but now everything seemed to me meaningless. In the morning, I had been in

33

Church for the Mass and in the afternoon, I had followed the procession, asking to the Saint to help and suggest me what I had to do. The night came down, I had no mind to go out among the happy and noisy crowd. I was sitting in the living room, full in my thoughts, bluffing a reading. My father had just come back from hunting and his carbine was placed in a corner, waiting to be put back. I reminded a day in which my father had explained how it works. "This is the cock, this the magazine and there you put the bullets..." he explained. "When you put off the safety lock, you must keep the barrel down". "Targeting is the most difficult thing. You need to keep the shotgun in this way; otherwise the recoil will push you back..." Adele came in, right in that moment: "Come on, Dress up. She said. Let's go out and see the stalls". Then, quietly, so that nobody could hear, she added: "Armando is waiting for you in the square, in front of the polar star. He wants to talk to you." I looked at her surprised and upset. I was scared; I did not want to meet him. "Go ahead", I said to Adele, "I will reach you in the square in few minutes."

I went in to my room, put on my best dress, the elegant shoes and I carefully combed my hair. Then I came back in the living room. My father and my mother were in the kitchen. I could hear them quarrelling about a land to buy. In a while, I got the shotgun and I ran down to the stairs. Before going out the door, I revised the shotgun bullets and put off the safety lock. The square was not so far, I walked in the darkness, keeping the shotgun upright, bordering on the houses. I was following my huge shadow, projecting on the walls, without seeing anything else around me. There was something pushing me, which lighted my steps, which gave me a sense of duty and obligation. A terrible desire of revenge and of payback

34

was growing inside my soul. Hot, fear and stress melted all together with my sweat, dripping from my hair, coursing down on my face, eyes, on my neck and on my shoulders. The light summer dress was soaked of water, as all my body. Suddenly, my anxiety vanished, leaving the place to a deep calm and an icy self-control. I quickly arrived around the bar, keeping myself at a short distance. He was there, in front of the doorway with a group of friends, smiling, smoking, joking, in his dark suit, with a matched tie and his usual self-confidence. I got closer shiftily, made the last steps quickly, and when I arrived few metres far, I pointed my shotgun. I saw him astonished and then, then I saw nothing else. A shot, two, three, four…My father was right; targeting is the most difficult thing. The explosion broke in the air and thundered in my brain, as exploded shells. Stunned, I crumpled against the wall, in a deep anxiety. Laughs, joy, chats that were echoing around, suddenly stopped and a leading silence lowered overall. Soon after that, a noise of broken glasses, fallen objects, people escape, screaming of fear, groans of pain, desperation, weeps and blood, blood everywhere, on the walls, on the pavement, on the tables…And then all those corps on the floors.

I am not afraid for him. It is not my business. He had a son, I know, but he had to think about it before. On the contrary, I was afraid for the other two youngers; they had nothing to deal with all. It had been a tragic fate, which put them on my path. I am sorry for the other one who is on wheelchair now, but I had to defend my honour. Even for that baby that I had given birth prematurely in prison, I am sorry. It has been a big sorrow, I had so many expectations on her, I would have seen her growing up, calling me Mum, coming and visiting me here and waiting for me at the exit. She would have been fifteen. She would have been a big support for me; she would have been the aim of my life".

Caserta, 1983

OLGA

"Yesterday, when I heard the screeching of the gate, closing beyond me, I had a panic and a shiver ran down my body. That metallic, sinister, unmerciful sound had showed me immediately the reality of that isolation cellar: dismal and bare, giving me a sense of segregation. The only one companion was the noise of a non-stop dropping water, falling down from the tap, counting down the seconds of time. I gave a glance around, grey walls, an iron bed, a run-down bedside table, a little wall unit and nothing else but desolation.

For the first time I became aware about the situation I had been living for all these years and now I am out of the whole world, closed here in, without nobody who can take care of me. The doubt I will not go out anymore was overwhelming me. The lawyer has been ambiguous; he did not guarantee me anything. I sent a telegram to my father but I do not know what will be his reaction. I have not seen my parents for many years. I was in conflict with them, I used to contrast them, and I could not stand their strictness.

My father was a rigid and authoritarian army officer, my mother a pragmatic and very little flexible teacher of maths. I hated their behaviour: hypocrite priggishness, conditioning them in each evaluation or action. Dreams, ideals were nothing but childish ingenuousness to confine in a world of improbability. The only one logic expectation was a plan of a certain job and an advantageous marriage. They thought love was the worst base for a long-term relationship, because, they argued, it is ephemeral and fleeting. "In choosing a husband, you need to consider above all his social prestige and economic solidity. Absolutely avoiding the handsome ones, because, it is well known, they are all Casanovas. Barren concept and lacking of any human quality, I have always believed. Saving your public reputation, you need to show your undeniable morality and solid wealth, as well as an unquestionable good taste.

I remember how many fights I made to dress a mini-skirt, to go to gym, to meet a group of friends with liberal ideas, in short to claim my personality and defend the right to choose autonomously. Leisure activities, hobbies, readings, cinema, theatre, all were smugly considered useless, with reproach, a waste of time, to practice with parsimony.

My sister Rosa and I were intolerant to that rigid atmosphere established at home; very different from that we could breathe in some our friends' families. My sister managed to escape from home, marring a wealthy but insignificant shopkeeper, who put her on a pedestal, laying down her feet in eternal devotion. I did not envy her. That was not my target; I was not going to spend the rest of my life in a golden cage, among children and cookers, playing rummy with friends, talking about fashion, recipes, or similar trifles. After Rosa's marriage, I felt alone. Even if we sometimes used to quarrel, she was a fellow, a friend for me. I put my heart and soul in studying and sports I preferred: swimming and volleyball. I have been always good at sport activities, so that, among my plans there was that of teaching or opening a gym. Maybe Sport gave me that harmony and the slender physical appearance, which men liked so much. I have never given too much importance to my charm. However, I felt proud and satisfied when in the street people turned back to admire me.

I was eighteen and I was attending last year of high school when I met Vittorio for the first time, just for chance. I tripped over a manhole, falling down clumsy, while my books slipped away down from my hands. In that moment, I regretted I could not avoid that ruinous slip, in spite of my agility conquered by my strenuous training. He helped me to rise up and to pick up my books, spread all over the pavement. He took me to the pharmacy to have my scraped knees disinfected and to the bar to let me pick up my spirit with a coffee. After that, he got me home by his brand new Mercedes Benz car. Flashed by his kindness and his gentle manners, I spent my following days thinking of him. He showed fifteen years more than I was, but his appearance was elegant and handsome, with an athletic body, very dark waving hair. He wore designed cloths and showed off great economic assets. After two days, I saw him again out of my school, waiting for me opposite to the gate. My heart lost a beat, but I bluffed calmness, while I walked closer, smiling. By that time, he used to come often out of school, to go around together in his car, talking or having a coke and then he got me home. He told me hardly nothing about himself. I only knew he came from a village near Vesuvius and that he had studied Economy at University, without getting his degree. His work activity was not clear; he was a cloth factory owner, with many workers, but he was also interested in Finance, building company and import –export business. I did not understand so much those things; he was only a businessperson for me.

He took me into an outlying flat, in a building, which witnessed an ancient but lost prestige, raising up among huge, popular and grey anonymous stocks of building. It was a quite bare and banal   little residence. Few ordinary furniture, no ornaments, carpets or other objects, which could characterize the environment. I felt upset, but I had enough braveness to ask him why such a rich man had a so lousy house. There I spent cheerful hours with him. I did not care anything but that love I felt growing inside my heart. We met very often, but sometimes he vanished for short periods for business. "I have to go to Milan for an agreement," he told me, or "I have been in Rome to meet an executive of the Ministry of public labour". Sometimes he went abroad, to the Netherlands, in particular, but the aim of travelling was always a mystery for me. He gave me his office telephone number, but I had rarely called him, I did not need to call him. He used to be the first to look for me, as soon as he could.

I felt completely conquered by his strong and determined personality, but I also noticed something mysterious and ambiguous in his behaviour, which upset me. His cryptic gaze was harsh and shining, like steel. I told him everything of my life, of my family, of my expectations, of my desire to emancipate from my parents, to become free and independent woman. He used to listen to me smiling with condescending manner. He had a controlling manner with me, deciding, establishing, acting for me and I used to accept that behaviour, as the normal consequence of our generation gap. His ripeness and his experience put him on a different level, to my eyes. He transferred me self-confidence and at the same time, he instilled fear. I almost did not dare to contradict him. Just for this, I had never asked him about his travels and his business. He liked high-powered car, he had more than one, which he changed repeatedly. He used to follow the race-cars and horses all over Italy. He was very busy and had many interests, I admired him a lot and his life-style seduced me.

He told me about diners, meetings with powerful and important people with whom he had worked and friendly relationships. I was proud of a man of this kind was giving me his time and attention and I felt happy when I saw his shining gaze looking at me. I knew I was not an occasional adventure for him. Despite of this, he had never had any plans for our future life.

One night, while he was taking me at home, stopped his car to buy cigarettes at the tobacconist. It was raining, I remained alone in that luxury car, while the continuous noise of the rain thundered on the car body, and the reflex of the passing car lights gave brightness to the street. Pushed by an instinctive curiosity, I opened the box of the dashboard and I found a dark oblong box, of a strange and mysterious shape. There was a big, shiny, dark, menacing revolver, which seemed new. I thought to have watched similar army only in movies. I was still keeping the revolver between my hands, with a worried and scared face, when he came back into the car. He did not show any perplexity. "It is a mean of defence, you have no idea how many criminals, robbers and thieves are all around". He said with a comforting smile. "Can you use it?" I ask scared. "Yes, of course. Otherwise, why do I need it?" He put the gun back into the box and that episode was completely forgot. Our relationship had been lasting for long, when he suddenly gave me a wonderful golden bracelet, studded by rubies and diamonds, without any reason or recurrent event in particular. It was his first gift and it was very precious. "I saw in a jewellery shop, and I thought of you. I could not help to buy it. I would cover you by gifts, but I know you couldn't show them at home," he said.

Few weeks after, while I was at school, my mother ransacked everywhere into my room, probably made suspicious by the fact I often went out in the afternoon. She found out the bracelet. At that point, I had to confess my secret, explaining I would have never given up that relationship I considered so important. Their predictable reaction was full of grudge and upset. They became sceptical. They wanted to meet him and understand what kind of person he was. I called him at the office, but nobody answered me. The clock said it was three o'clock in the afternoon and maybe the secretary had not finished her lunch break yet. I had to see Vittorio and tell him what had happened, and we had to decide what we have to do. I found myself in a terrible state of anxiety; I could not foresee how he would have reacted to the inevitable stubbornness of my parents. I knew he could not stand any kind of stubborn. At four o'clock I decided to go to his office. I was too nervous to wait for long. I had never been in that office before; I did not know where it was.

From the doorway, I saw a woman coming out. She was showy, fair, with a deep make up, she had a sluttish appearance and she seemed clearly angry. She went away without noticing me. I came in, giving my name to the secretary, saying I urgently needed to see Vittorio. "I don't know if he will receive you. He has just quarrelled with his wife". She exclaimed ironically, pointing to the exit. I spent many days closed in my room, crying, damning my naivety and my evil fate. I understood the reason of such strange behaviours and many other particular signs I had not examined with the right attention. I had sworn everything in that love, which in short became a passion, so that I considered it as determining for my life and now it seemed everything could collapse down as sand castle. I felt anguished by my mother's manner, who gazed me with a mix of worrying and reproaching, regretting not to have transferred me her ideas and principles. She recognised that event as a betrayal and her failure, trying to talk to me, disarmed in front of my desperation. At home, there was a high and deep stressed atmosphere, even because my exam for high school diploma became very close and my frame of mind was not good at facing with such an important exam.

Weeks had passed since that day, when an evening, coming out from the gym I saw Vittorio's car, stopped at the corner. The emotion tied my throat up. I tried to find my self- composure, meaning to pour over him all angry I had inside, but when he got closer I couldn't utter any word and I melted in a river of tears, because of my angry and sadness. He swore his marriage had already ended long time before, and he was waiting for divorce and he could not do without me, anymore. The whole grudge I had inside melted as fog under the sunlight, his love for me represented the only important thing. He faced me with a choice: leaving each other or going to live together, waiting for our marriage after getting the divorce. I had to make up my mind, but even if next days I was so uncertain and full of doubts, I could not take any kind of clear decision. Surely, my parents would have never accepted a cohabitation with a man, married, moreover. On the other hand, I didn't want to leave everything and venture throughout a difficult path, even if I realized that Vittorio had become more and more an essential part of my life.

The fate decided for me. I found out to be pregnant and the choice became a duty. It was late in the night when I collected few things, waited my parents were asleep and I went forever away, far from that house I was born. I didn't know what would my future be , where would I go to live, how would my life be and I didn't know I would never come back to my village. He brought me in a close city. He bought a wonderful mansion in a luxury garden in a residential area. A park dived into the green, with buildings surrounded by basins and gushing fountains, flowered gardens and well neat grasslands, across by tree-lined walkways. A daydream residence with open- lighted spaces, elegant and well refining furniture. A glass- sliding doorway opened into a bid sitting room, with mirrored marble floor. A series of decorated glass divided the spaces, while a fine wooden stair went up to the bedrooms. It was more than I could wish. I was running around those rooms as Alice in the Wonderlands, astonished by so much magnificence. I hugged him strongly and he sweetly caressed my hair, smiling at me. Our life together had started there, even if, to say the truth, we had never been together. He came, then he went away for days, he came back and then he left again, always busy for work, business travels and every kind of commitment.

He provided me a fellow; I could not stay alone in my condition. Clorinda was a young woman coming from Torre Annunziata, sturdy, dynamic, always cheerful. He made several jobs, housekeeper, governess, assistant or all-rounder. She had been a valid supporter, even if I had always suspected she had the task to control me. Coming from a humble family, her mother was housewife and his father was a carpenter, very close to Vittorio for unknown reasons. Clorinda, a very young woman, had had a singular experience of which she had spoken little and reluctantly. At the age of sixteen, she had a strong religious calling and went into a nunnery. Her family disagreed that decision, but never impeded her. After the novitiate, when she had to take the vows, suddenly she realized to have made a mistake, leaving the nunnery, for reasons she had never revealed. So, she was quite a nun, and Vittorio considered her liable because she had a mix of moral and personal qualities of efficiency and reliability.

Vittorio had never lacked me anything but his presence. In that period, my existence was always the same, without any human meetings, except for some acquaintances, who, moreover, were distrustful towards me. I had the sensation to live in a temporary situation, not yet defined which would have been soon changed after his divorce.

I had no more relationship with my parents. They had never forgot me for that escape, seen as an insult. My sister, on the contrary, often used to call me to update me on familiar news, and she seldom came to visit me. I used to spend my time in waiting, planning my future and my son's. Male or female, he/she would attend the best school, thanks to her/ his father economical means. I would not think to save money for my child's education, for foreign languages studying, for holyday camps abroad. I would follow him step by step in his growing, giving him the suitable tools for his physical and mental development, with the right range of freedom for his personality growth. I would not limit his expectations and I would give him the chance to realize his intellectual skills in the best way.

Luca arrived early, during an icy rainy night, in December, very close to Christmas. I had unexpected birth pains and Clorinda, efficient and active as always, brought me to the hospital. The labour was long and painful, but when I could hold in my arms that little lonely and vulnerable creature, it seemed I received a gift from God and I immediately forgot every sufferance. He strongly cried and his little hands strongly held mine

45

as in a searching of help. Only my caresses and my kisses kept him calm. In that very moment, I knew my life would be indissolubly linked to his forever.

Vittorio came after few hours and he was happy, but more when he noticed he had his same features and colours, as willing, dark eyes and skin. He stayed with me few days. He waited for my recovery, my coming back home, than he left again. He came at Christmas, bestowed a luxurious, large, warm and elegant sable fur coat upon me. I brushed that soft, shiny, fawn fur of that useless present, while I was listened to his important business agreement he had recently done, receiving a big profit. He emphasized his already bought golden Rolex watch, showing his wrist as well as his new burning Ferrari, he proudly used to come to me, as trophies won for a battle. Another luxurious car to add to his car parking, already well furnished. It seemed to me an excess. It was just in that very moment that I started to look at me differently. Maybe being mother had given me a new criticism, which I had not before. I suddenly glimpsed what I had never seen before, an empty personality, an extreme consumer attitude, which gave too importance to material interests, neglecting the most important values of life. Money, which could open every door, was the aim he pursued and the means he used to realize his dreams, otherwise he could not reach, and to follow impossible and far illusions. My son was my only most important aim of life. I looked at him and I felt a strong emotion, a compulsive desire to protect him, to keep him away out of hardship and meanness of human beings. As a fool, I wished he could never grow up, pretending not to see him facing with the unavoidable obstacle of the existence.

Vittorio was always busy; sometimes I saw him nervous, anxious and worried. He spoke at phone with unknown people, with low voice and broken sentences. Often, after a call, he went quickly away, because of urgent concerns, as an excuse. Time passed, but his divorce was more and more away, and with it, the possibility to legalize our relationship. "There are thousands problems, difficulties. It needs more time, but you'll see: everything will be ok" he said.

Luca was growing up beautiful, clever, lively, creative and curious, as all the children. He took all my time, my love, my interest. He loved his father; he represented a myth for him, an idol, and his hero. Maybe because he saw him so rarely or maybe because Vittorio was an able seller of himself. When the baby was three years old, he went to nursery school. Clorinda took care of the house, as usual, and I found more time for myself. Therefore, I decided to follow a course for aesthetician. I considered it an interesting, modern activity, concerning my attitude. Vittorio showed enthusiasm to the idea, and as soon as I got my diploma, he opened for me a cutting-age beauty centre for me in a central area of the town. During those years, I had been lived a normal life: I used to take care of Luca; I used to go out with some friends until the job inside the beauty centre have given me time. It gave me a great deal of effort. Customers were kind but hard to please, as all those who pay.

He was my husband, even if we were not married, but for me he was as a husband. I saw no difference. It was an illusion, indeed. That mysterious, talented and full of secrets man had never showed me his real soul. He had never broken that deep veil under which he used to unravel the string of his life. Something behind his steel eyes of an icy glaze let me suspect a

47

completely different reality from the showed one. On Luca's birthday, in a pocket of my husband's jacket I found the bill of a double room in a hotel of Rome. The excuse he added was credible: "there were no single room available and I took a double one". I know it was a lie. Some of his behaviour, gestures, words, nothing concrete, only ambiguous, invisible elements made me understand I was not the only woman in his life. It was only a feeling, I kept hide in the secret of my life.

During summertime, he brought us to the sea. He bought a flat in at the seaside on the Domitian area. It was a comfortable flat, very close to the beach, with a beautiful balcony, where our baby could play freely. It was there where I found I little plastic bag full of white powder, carefully hidden among boxes and parcels, enveloped by packaging paper. I stayed stunned for long, looking at that unequivocal prohibit substance, which coursed among my fingers. It was a huge quantity, maybe more than a kilo. I wondered how many doses could have been done from it, how many people could have been killed, how much money you could get from it. Trepidation and heartbeat overwhelmed me, I was sweaty and my heart was heavy like a millstone. That discovery showed to my eyes a scene I had not even remotely imagined. Where those his affairs? Was that the way he used to get money to live and let me live in luxury? Was that the man I loved and I had been living with? I remembered the gun I had found in the dashboard of his car few years before, which now he did not worry about hiding it. Therefore, I wondered if he had never used it, why and against whom. Behind a mask of a handsome man, a businessperson, a lovely father there was an unknown being, overpowered by the devil of corruption. When he came back from the beach, I was in bed, ill, but I did not explain the reason. I said nothing. I was afraid to speak and above all, at that point I was afraid to know. I realize that my behaviour has been ambiguous, maybe even incoherent. I had to leave him, but I did not know where I could go, and I was not sure at all, he would accept my decision, without contrasting me. Sincerely I did not want to lose all I had: my wealthy and comfortable life, my luxurious house, the house at the beach, the beauty centre, the expensive car, my current account, and therefore, compelling my son to give up all his wealth, in which he was born. I had fit myself to the situation. I pretended to ignore, I tried not to know, even if Vittorio knew that I had realized everything.

Time had passed in an atmosphere of compromise, of uncertainty and great anxiety. He had been recently nervous, worried more than ever; he jumped at a phone or doorbell ringing, smoked too much, and flipped nervously the pages of newspaper or listened carefully the TV news; it seemed that he was waiting for an impressive news or a striking event at any time.

Last Tuesday I Picked up Luca at school. He attends the second year of the primary school. We came back home and I switched the TV on, while I was preparing the dinner. Clorinda had gone to her village for a couple of days. All at once, a baby's astonishing exclamation made me freeze: "Mum, Look: there is dad on TV!" I saw on the TV screen Vittorio's photo while the impersonal speaker's voice was explaining: "This morning, in a street in Rome Vittorio C., a little Industrial business man of Vesuvius area and right hand man of the well-known Boss R.C., leader of the Camorra organization, had died together with his lover inside his own car after an unexpected explosion. Details of the fact are not clear yet, it

49

has not been stated if the huge quantity of TNT which provoked the explosion, had been brought by Vittorio himself to make an attack or it had been strategically placed inside his car to kill him. His role inside the criminal organization was well known for long time, but the detectives had never found any proof, which showed his criminal affairs or illegal traffics". Trembling, I dragged away Luca far from TV, but he cried to know everything, because he did not understand; I did not know how to get him calm, I was scared and in turn, he gazed me scared too. "Mum, what happened to Dad?" He asked imploring me. The investigation, the searching, the questioning and interviews of the last days had destroyed me. Nothing was found at home. He would never leave some compromising document or illicit objects, but the fact we were leaving together was a concrete data, they had found my name in someone's diary, and we both owned the properties. They are convinced I know something, that I could give them some names, they think I was his partner in crimes, in such a way…". Caserta 1983.

ROSA

The stomping notes of Ravel's Bolero had been spreading in the air, clear and overwhelming, while I was coming in the gym, where about ten prisoners were rhythmically training. Rosa was there, with her eyes fixed in the emptiness, looking without seeing her friends, who were moving with synchronic gestures. She had perfect features; she was thin and slim, with amber skin and glossy long dark hair. She gave me a melancholic and gloomy gaze. "I was arrested yesterday", she said. "I know it would happen. Police had been investigating on me for months; my life had been put through the wringer. They were stubbornly looking for something. My existence, you know, is like an abstract painting: with spots, distorted profiles and shadowing zones. People say that everyone is the creator of his own fortune, but I have never done so much to build up my destiny in such absurd way. Everything had happened involuntary and I had found myself in this hard path without my awareness. I was a normal girl until a dramatic event happened into my life, messing it up.

I was eighteen when it happened. I was like many other girls at that age, idealistic and unprepared. I attended my third year of high school, with many boys who were competed for the pleasure to go along with me until the bus stop. When I met Mauro, all the others disappeared; nobody could compete with him, to my eyes. He was handsome, intelligent and nice, always with an ironic attitude, which gave him the idea of an awesome easy-going boy. He attended the same school of mine, the last year. He had many girls who were following him in love, barraged him with letters, messages and calls. However, he did not care about it enough. He used to smile coldly to everyone, never pledging with no one of them. I often saw him at the five a side football field, near my house, playing with his friends. I used to look at him for hours, hidden behind the window glass, but I bluffed to ignore him and he seemed to ignore my existence, too. One day I met him in the street. He was riding his moped when he stopped asking me if I wanted a lift. I climbed up behind him and we never more separated. I wished I spent with him all the moments of my days, listening to his voice, keeping his secrets, understanding his thoughts. When he was far, I felt I get lost, feeling a deep sense of emptiness. He was happy with me. I could see that in his gazes, in his way to speak and smile at me. His feelings were like mine: clear and honest. It seemed nothing could cloud our perfect harmony.

His family was rich but rustic, made up of people who gave importance to appearance and to gossip. His father was a good and nice man, without education but very intelligent and experienced. He was a good builder and he had set up a good company. His mother was small minded, full of condescension, without qualm, ready to trash everyone, just to get her targets. She resorted to a low trick in order to marry her husband: she bluffed a pregnancy. On the contrary, the baby born more than a year after the marriage. He endured her; he could not stand her manners, looking for his solace among several lovers' arms. That woman developed a deep and incomprehensible aversion towards me. I think she was jealous of me, as all mothers are, and maybe she couldn't stand his only male child was in love with a poor, humble and orphan girl, who could never add or give prestige to her family. She tried to impede our love and she used very kind of pretext to impede our meetings. On the contrary, my mother had never tried to control me. Maybe because she thought I was enough self-confident or just because she was too weak to face with such a rebel daughter, intolerant to every type of hypocrisy and conformism.

She was a modest woman, got used to work and to sacrifice, in particular after my father's death. She used to speak very little, making few questions, but she understood everything. She knew about Mauro and about his mother's aversion towards me. Even if she had never prevented me, she had often suggested stopping that relationship. However, Mauro became my stable, important representative of my life. I spent almost all of my afternoons with him, riding his moped in the streets, listening to music and talking in my bedroom. We could talk for hours about thousands of unlimited topics. In the evening we often went to the cinema, or to some place set apart, where we could stay together alone, without being disturbed. We used to go to a romantic and quite place. A green hill, full of poplars and oaks, which overlooked a valley made up of cottages, fields and vineyards. The street to get there was prickly and curvy. However, on the top, the atmosphere was calm and the silence was stopped only by birds' twitter. I liked watching out the sunset from there, behind the horizon line.

That day of June we went there at the nightfall, the air around was warm and clam; sitting on the grass we were quietly talking. Suddenly three masked people appeared at once; they had their faces covered by a ski -mask, which allowed only their eyes half seen. They seemed criminals; I thought they wanted to steal us. Besides, they came for something else. They were frightful, dark, untrustworthy and sneaky shadows. I will never forget the cruel and fierce gaze of one of them, as a wild beast. He wore a violet ski mask, which underlined his little and menacing eyes. They tied Mauro to a tree and they had raped me several times, all the three, for hours. Nobody could help us; nobody could hear our scream, my painful groans, nor his invectives. It had been a terrible never- ending nightmare. They ran away after two hours, when we could hear a noise of car. The lights of the car blinded me; a sliver of white light pointed on my face was my release. I was shocked, covered by bruises, wounds, abrasions, dirty of blood, sweat and mud. I had been recovered into the hospital for four days where I had my body wounds healed, but not those of my soul.

When I came out I realized I was completely alone, without no more friends, who avoided me as I was an infected, and I hadn't Mauro anymore. Maybe I did not look for him, for not digging up that terrible reminder, on maybe it was he, I do not know, surely our paths divided forever. I was told that he had suffered a lot and that experience signed him deeply, but then, he had forgot everything. On the contrary, me, How I could forget it? I had always been obsessed by a doubt in my brain; a perverse doubt had consumed my mind for years, the doubt that behind that fact there were Mauro's mother sneaky plans. She was a person capable of such an action of this type. I had no proof of that, only a terrible suspicion, which was quietly spreading all over the village, after all. My mother was the only one who stood by me, as a shadow who was following me loyal and silently. She did not bring me up anything, but sometimes her gaze was heavier than a millstone. When Michele started to pursue me, he well knew my story; everyone knew it.

Five years had spent from that terrible night, and my life was going on grey and boring. He was forty, and he was the owner, together with his brothers of a big building material society, enough talked about, which was standing up thanks to illegal business of various kind. Maybe just for this reason he never left apart his gun, a little army, which he always took with him. He was thin, dark, with ordinary physical appearance, with sharp cornered features. He wore expensive cloths. All he owned was expensive: his car, watch, lighter, glasses, pen. He smiled in an incomprehensible way and when he spoke to me, he put his gaze elsewhere. As a young man, he had been the typical bully bluster of the village. As the time passed he put right in his head; he married and he carried on his too old father's business; he knew Mauro's family and it was well known in the village that in the past he had received a conspicuous loan to avoid finance disarray. I would not notice him in other circumstances.

Even if he was rich, he had a measly soul and I felt very lonely, always deluding myself into finding some affection towards me. His marriage was in failure, saved only by his wife's ability to hold up silently his oppression and betrayals. He was arrogant and assertive, but he deftly disguised his character, bluffing generous and kind. He showed off his richness without reserve and without any style, he used to shower me with presents, taking me out for dinner in elegant places or in luxurious hotels for some weekends outwards.

Then, he soon changed his behaviour and his real personality came out clearly. It happened when he noticed my fondness for Gianni. Gianni worked in my uncle Renato's laboratory who owns a big patisserie in the inner city of Caserta. It is a very famous patisserie and on Sunday morning, half city uses to queue out of the shop to buy lemon tarts, jam tarts, the famous special "pastiera". Gianni was his assistant. He was not handsome, but when he smiled, he had something appealing which gave him allure. There was a good feeling between us. A simple word was enough to understand each other or to laugh or even to feel astonished about the same thing. He was still a boy; he had been working for my uncle since his father's death. His father was a sales clerk, with a big portfolio at the time of his accident that caused his death. Gianni was the elder son and he had to leave school to help his family. Maybe just for this reason he seemed always sad and lost in his thoughts. I liked Gianni and Gianni liked me, it was clear, but sometimes there was something ambiguous in his gaze, which scared me. Michele hated him, he saw him as a rival, even if he never confessed it. He became jealous and possessive, pretending I went out only with him, waiting at home his calls. He used violence and humiliations to submit me to his will. He wanted to decide everything of my life, he considered me as his personal object.

Our relationship had been lasting for two years by that time, and I became intolerant towards his manners, towards his arrogance and his rude soul. I should have got rid of him, but I could not, something was preventing me to do it, I do not know what. He stuck on me as a sucker. He kept me tied up by menaces, blackmails, expensive gifts; he did not realize he let my aversion growing inside me, in that way. Maybe it was me, I could not love anyone else, and by that time and I became dry, cheap of feelings. Surely, the memory of that night never went away from my mind. None of the days in my life had spent without tears, remembering that horrific scene and those cruel and perverse eyes gazing me with greediness. Who knows what could be the result of such traumatic experience for an eighteen years old girl's soul?

For next summer holidays, Michele had rent a little flat in in the suburb of Sorrento, part of a block of houses recently restored, a beautiful park, full of flowerbeds. The area was desert and silently. You seldom could meet someone throughout the stairs or in the pathways. The little flat was all white painted, with limited spaces and essential furniture. A typical summer flat he had rent to stay alone together with me. We often went there when he was free. We spent our mornings on the beach taking long baths into the sea, and sunbathing. At night, it was funny walking among the luxurious shop windows in the centre or having dinner into one of the many typical and refined places there. Sorrento is wonderful, so different from that little hidebound village in which I was forced to live, a village with gossipy and blabbermouth people, always ready to judge and to censure. Nevertheless, even the trips in Sorrento became intolerable: he always nagged at me with his jealously and my intolerance grew in excess.

One day Michele never came back home, he disappeared and nobody saw him anymore. His car was founded early in the morning in a little country path in the suburb of the village, with keys still in the dashboard. It was improbable he spontaneously went far away; he did not take with him clothes, documents, nor left messages or contacted anybody. His relatives were confused, discouraged, they did not know what to thing about. His wife came twice at home; she knew our relationship, which was known by everyone. She was looking for some detail that could justify his disappearing. My mother let her get in. She told her I could not give her any news about her husband, let her understand, kindly that her visits were

57

no more appreciated. I did not let her see me; I did not want to meet her. Then, police started to investigate. His disappearing was soon considered odd. They thought about a case of "Lupara Bianca", that is a way of killing without leaving a trace.

However, unravelling the knot was not easy; his business matters were often anything but clear and he had relationship with people of all type, many of them were good for nothing. The police interviewed friends, enemies, acquaintances, relatives, employees and at the end, they came to me. I could not give any detail; I said that the day of his disappearance and the day before I had always been at home, I did not meet him at all. They went away very little persuaded by my statements. The investigation concentrated on an employee of the Company, who was suspected he had stolen money from the company cash register, but nothing was proved. They arrived in France, too, where he often went to meet a business friend, and even in that case nothing emerged.

The researches arrived at an idle time. Many times I wondered what would have happened if they had found it. I spent my night sleepless, toss and turn, awake in the bed in a state of anxiety and days were passing waiting for news, in the hope that something concrete would come out and the stressful waiver would finish soon. I felt as dived in a nightmare, looking at everything from the above, without any chance to be at. I was waiting for something serious would happen. Among his documents, they had found the tenancy of the house in Sorrento, which they had checked many times, and maybe they found something. They investigate the toll payments types at the Motorway operator, too, and even there, they found something. Then, one morning they came to me. They were four police officers, who showed me a search warrant. My mother stunned, her face was a sad bitter mask. Sitting in a corner, she was looking astonished at those people who were ransacking and searching everywhere, without saying a word. The house was completely turned upside down; my room and that of my mother were minutely inspected. That infringement of personal effects, that exploring and scanning among objects and things, made me felt terribly upset and deeply hurt me. I could see my mother's linen, the family's photos, letters and documents, turned upside down without respect, as trash.

Anxious and suspicious, they were sniffing the air as bulldogs, searching a sign or a clue. It seemed they grope around, searching inside the wardrobe, in the sideboard, inside drawers, in the pockets of the clothes, inside bags, but we did not understand what they were looking for, nor did they know it. They were going away, disgruntled and dissatisfied, when crossing the courtyard, they saw an old well, dismissed and completely dry. It is ancient, bare stoned, an historical relic. They moved close to it, with wariness, nearly scared. They picked up the top and looked inside it the green musk and smelly mould, which covered the wall, and the firm, rotten mud, placed on the bottom. The emerging of undetectable shadow made them suspicious. They took ropes, stairs, pulleys, and someone went down into the deep. They had to work hard to pick out the suitcase. It was a big brown leather suitcase, heavy and swelled up and well locked. When they picked it up on the surface, they became all speechless and astonished. They carefully opened it, fearing the worst. As a matter of the fact, they found the huddled and wrinkled Michele's body inside, by then, in a forward state of decay. I could feel everyone's astonishing gazes upon me. I would have not killed him. It had happened all at once, without I could realize it. That very day we had argued. The reason is useless, after all. He would have liked to make love with me, but I did not want. We had just arrived in, and we were in the bedroom. He was terribly angry and hit me by a couple of slaps. I went back instinctively and gazed him, straight into his eyes. It was just in that very moment that I saw the same sullen greed glance of that night. Those little and evil eyes which the violet ski mask let them glimpsed.

How was it possible? Several suspects became to shake inside of my soul. Was he that man? Was it only a suggestion? How was it possible I had never noticed him? Was it the reason of his elusive glaze? I analysed his body: even the other one was little and thin, maybe, but perhaps it was a hallucination.

The upset expression on my face bewildered him, he gazed me confused, I stunned for a while, then with a jerk I got closer to the night stand, , where the gun was , always handily. I lightning grasped it, took off the safety lock and pointed it against him. A light anxiety painted his face. "What do you want to do?" he asked me with a reconciling smile: "Do you want to scary me?" "No" I answered. "I want to kill you". Two shots were enough, two tragic deflagrations, which thundered all over the house. I stunned with my arm already stretched, while I was looking at him, falling down on the floor. I set on the bed, with the gun in my hand, contemplating astonished his motionless body, folded and contracted in his last spasm, lying on the floor, at few steps from me. His astonished expression printed on his bloodiness face. A bullet had to hit him straight to the heart; the other went lower, maybe to the spleen. His light skirt became red, with a rivulet of blood, flowing fast, colouring the floor. I got slowly down the gun and then I waited. Of course, many people would come in, hearing the shoots. The noise had thundered into the silence of that area, leaving a deafen echo.

It seemed impossible that no one had listened to it. I stood waiting for the events. All at once, someone would knocked at the door, maybe the police, alerted by neighbours. I was thinking about the cause of all that. What would I say to exonerate myself from that? "I had the suspicion he was one of those who had raped me many years ago..." as excuse it did not hold up at all. I would say he wanted to kill me, and I could get and grasp the gun before him, but even that excuse was improbable, it would be difficult to demonstrate it. Maybe It was better to say he mistreated and hit me it was less believable. I had no bruises, nor signs of bush and then it was not a suitable excuse. While I was making up my mind, time passed and nothing happened. I wondered I was facing that odd situation with such a detachment and coldness. It seemed I was acting a dramatic film, as in a while all would be finished, lights would be switched off and someone would have said: "Stop! The scene is finished." On the contrary, I was there, deep in that tragic nightmare, waiting for someone or something, which did not arrive. No one came in, no one was interested, no one asked, no one had heard. When the night came down, I decided to go away. I put the gun inside Michele's trousers pocket; I put him off his shoes. Then I folded carefully his body, trying to let it placed inside the suitcase. It was a very large, strong and handily suitcase. Then, without many difficulties, I closed the zip. His wallet remained out, but it did not seem to me a big problem. I would have destroyed few days after. I carefully cleaned all the house and the bloody spots disappeared. I dragged the suitcase to the car, which was close to the house; I put it inside the boot, I started the car up and I went towards the village. It was dark in the night and the place was desert. Oddly, I was not tired nor stressed, and, in spite of the terrible adventure, I could feel determination and great energy. At the tollbooth in Caserta, the south exit, I paid using Michele's card I had found inside his pocket, so that the toll collector could not recognize me. When I arrived inside the courtyard I threw the suitcase into the well, then I brought the car in a country path and I went back home on foot. It was few minutes to four o'clock. I felt calm enough, no one saw me, but the card had betrayed me.

Police had controlled it and they stated the using of the card just on 21 August in Castellammare di Stabia, deducing that very day Michele went to Sorrento and next morning, at 2.40, his car got off the tollbooth in Caserta. After few hours, at 5.47 the car was found abandoned in a country path. I had declared that the day of missing, the 21 of August I did not meet him at all, but that day he was in Sorrento and he could be there only with me, I was the only one person who could know what had happened the next night when the car was again in the village. Now I cannot imagine what will happen. The investigators are looking for an accessory: they say I could not have done all by myself, they think about my mother or even Gianni. The worry upset me, moreover the doubt: Was he really one of the three men of that night on the hill? The man with the violet ski mask who filled in my nightmares? Maybe that ghost will haunt me all my life, hiding beyond all men's glaze I will meet.

Caserta, 1987

CLAUDIA

"Yesterday the psychologist told me that my personality is weak, fragile, and easy to influence and to manipulate, less provided of self-defence tools and disposed to self-destruction. All bullshits. Nobody had manipulated me. For what concerns the self-destruction it seems to me a real big pile of crap. I didn't really want to destroy myself; I only was in search of news".

She has a shameless gaze, Claudia, with a scrawny appearance, shrunken skin, but with also a powerful voice and aggressive manners. Her energy is concentrated only on her words, she speaks repeatedly, always, without a pause, and she listens to people very few, and reluctantly.

"There is not always a logic explanation to what you do; the reasons are hidden, incomprehensible. I do not know the reasons of what I have done; of course, I would not expect to be here. I only wanted to have fun, to flout, and I wanted to try it. There was a lot of it, around at your fingertip and I wanted to try it. After all, what the hell was wrong of it? Well, it is true; I saw many friends damned screwed for the withdrawal, loss of appetite, hallucinations, indolence, but I was sure I would have never had the same destiny, I would have never got injured of it. "I had told to myself: now I want to try a little bit of it, then, I will decide; if I like it, I will get a fix every fifteen days, no more". On the contrary, I immediately got it harshly, not like some who start with hashish, the aspirin into Coke, Roipnol into wine, all bullshits. I started with the heroin, it was easy, I had seen the others and I did the same. I took a rectangle of paper, I rolled it on, shaping a dropping funnel, I put a tip into a naris, I closed the other, and I inhaled the dust. At the beginning, I followed Walter's advice, my boyfriend in that period, and I started with a little quantity. I was sixteen, with a great craving for raising hell. Then, instead, I found trip funny, the travelling in the unreal world made me feel euphoric and immortal. That sublime flight was fantastic. It made me feel light as a butterfly, which flies into the air over the mediocrity reality of everyday life. Therefore, I became addicted, shit! However, creating that flight became soon too much expensive, much more then styled clothes, which till that moment I had pretended from my mother.

When she knew it, it had passed nearly a year from the very first time. I had taken heroin into vein, and I had already collected a good experience in theft, robbery and bag- snack. Selling out my body, I could earn much more. I had a big crowd out of the door, but men were disgusting; they were stinky, drunk, sweaty, sticky, all peppers and perverted, asshole people! I preferred stealing, after all, it was funny and the adrenalin rose to the top. It was not difficult. Walter and I stopped an old fool woman in the street, we threatened her with a knife to terrify her just a little and we tore her bag away, before she could start to think about. Otherwise, we got in a shop, during a death time, when there were no customers and while Walter was pointing the toy gun towards the owner or shop assistant's temple, I emptied out the cash register.

Soon after that, we ran away in a twinkling among the little streets of the town. One day in a shit jewellery the burglar alarm went off. The doors locked and we were fucked, stopped inside with the toy gun in our hand, as two cocks. They arrested us, but they realised us soon, we were underage. When my mother came and took me at the police station, she made an endless tragedy. "Why did you do it? Why do you use drugs? Are there any problem at school? Has your father's death traumatized you? Is the guilt mine because I could not educate you well? All questions of shit, good only to fed up the loo. I have done it only because I wanted and stop, I wanted to try it. After all, I have already had everything I could wish; fashion style clothes, the stereo, the Sector watch, the moped, the study holiday in London every year, the holydays in Sardinia. I did not matter of other things.

My mother and I have been living together for many years, me, always looking for money to buy drug, and her, searching a way to make me stop at it. She made me stay in a clinic, where for a month they cured me with intravenous feeding, psychotherapy, psychiatric drugs, massages, Turkish bath and similar bullshits. Who knows how much she spent. It would be better to give me that money. As soon as I went out of the clinic, I took it up soon again, that very same day. I could not help it. Then, she made me recover inside a community, a drug rehabilitation centre. From there, I ran away after three days. It was impossible to live inside it. Better the prison, here is better, shit! They woke us up at five and they made us work as slaves all the daylong in the fields, taking care of cows and hens. It was whooping freeze and we were always between mud and dung. How gross! We ate very little and very bad. At nine, we were already in the bed. Then, always doing the group therapy, where everyone was confiding, confessing, regretting, mending themselves' way. Ginormous bullshits, which can make even Little Red riding hood laugh. I do not regret; I do not mend myself way. I like heroin, and I will always take it. Of course, here I cannot buy it. Do not think you had detoxified me. Mine is a mental addiction. My unconscious thought comes always back to that fly; hidden inside my brain, there is a silent fire, which will never extinguish. When I am out, even after fifteen years, the first thing I do will be a dose. My mother took me to an exorcist, too, to a nun, to a saint, to other several frauds, shit cheats, who got out a lot of money from her. She was ready to give money to everyone, everyone but me, what a bitch! Lately, she seemed to have given up.

On the contrary, three months ago a bad fact happened. I wanted money, but she started again: "you are giving up yourself, what will your life be? Why don't you stop it? I am dying desperate, watching my daughter who is destroying herself…". She didn't want to stop talking… I didn't care about what she was talking about, I only wanted money and I told her it. "I don't care a shit about destroying myself, I don't care a shit of my life! I don't care a shit you are dying; I want my drug and nothing else."

But she was continuing, she didn't understand and she didn't give me money. We were in the kitchen. On a shelf, I saw a set of knives which my father had bought. There were a lot of them, of different sizes and then I took one of them and I put inside her, under her ribs.

Fortunately, she didn't die. Otherwise who knows how many years I would be compelled to stay here inside. But she had her spleen and a piece of intestine got away. Yesterday she came to speak to me for the first time. she was very bad, a shit, pale, thin, get old, a little depressed, I felt a little sorry for her. She told me she forgives me, that I will be always her daughter, whatever I do, and she loves me. During the trail, she will help me and when I get out, she will help me to detoxify myself in every way.

Always the same story. She will never learn. But what is there to forgive? I didn't want to kill her. It was a bullshit. It was an angrily gesture, maybe exaggerate, but involuntary gesture. I know my addiction crisis destroy my will, taking me in the bed, suffering from muscular contractions, with stomach contractions, shaking by shivers of coldness and impulses to vomit. I know all of that, soon or late will take me to the end, but I will never adapt myself to live a boring painful and hardly life you live".

Arienzo, 1990

TERESA

Teresa looked out the metal grill of gate, while I was walking along the hallway of the prison section and she greeted, smiling at me. She was of those habitual detainees, one of those who, making frequent crimes came repeatedly into prison for more or less long periods of time.

She was a pretty shapely girl, with long and thick brown hair, falling down covering her shoulders. I saw her a little fade, a little fat, with a little but clear scar on her forehead. Her gaze was lifeless and her wasted face had some dark shadows under her eyes.

"What did you do this time?" I asked. "Nothing, Doc". She answered. "Have they arrested you for nothing?" "Nothing is not right...a pickpocketing...at the shopping centre, but with my habitual lucky, what could I find inside the wallet? Three thousand lire (Italian currency before Euro's introduction n.d.t) and a lottery ticket expired. The police were there and they found me immediately". "Why don't you get your head together and find a job?" "What kind of job could I find? I have always done it in my life, since I was a child. I had always stolen. I can do only that.

We were six children in my family, two females and four males. We lived in a slum, only one dark humid room, with little old and beaten-up furniture. You could never see the sun. Throughout the roller shatters, always lowered down, a pale light seeped inside, clouded by the shadow of the buildings nearby. We slept piled; we ate when it was possible. We never washed; the hygiene was a luxury, as many other things. I have never gone to school. I went around the street of Naples dirty, barefoot, untidy, together with my brothers and other poor children like us. We stole whatever or whomever we went across, we were a band of hungry and wild helpless, and people called us "little evils".

Once we attacked a little girl of our same age, more or less. I remember her frightened expression, her tears on her face, pale as the beeswax, her imploring eyes, gazing us; she had a gold necklace, lightening at the sun, it seemed of great value and we pursed snatch it in a flash and we ran away. The money we received from my father's friend dealer was not enough even to buy a candy for each of us.

My father was disabled unemployed, he was lacking of a leg, he had lost it stepping on a mine on fields, soon after the war, and despite of his conditions he was a hardened crook. Playing on people's piety he managed to fool everybody, doctors, lawyers, police officers and even priests. One day, after his own confession, he ransacked all the boxes inside the empty church. He had been often in prison and my sister and I brought him cigarettes and clean linen, but they let him out soon, because of his disability. My mother whored, but she did not earn very much, maybe because she was not so charming. As a matter of the fact, customers were extremely rare.

Money had never been enough at home. Too many mouths to feed, so that, as soon we could go away, everyone went out on his own life. I had lost my contacts with some of my brothers, nor do I know how and where they are living. Besides, I often meet my brother Nicola. We are strongly tied. When he is in prison, I often meet him during the jail talks and I bring him the food pack. Now, however, he has been transferred to Sardinia for quite long time, in a special security jail. They gave him the 41 bis (special law sentence for special crimes T.n) which means strict regime prison, a sort of metaphor to say you are fucked: no touch with the outside. I have always known he would be successful in his career; he would become an important person. There, visiting him was not so easy. You had to across the sea and the travel was long and expensive. I cannot do so much for him now. Sometimes I send him a telegram or a postcard with few words to say him hallo. I cannot send him letters because I am illiterate: I cannot write and he cannot read.

At the age of fifteen, I started my mother's same job, then, when I met Anacleto, I went to live with him. Of course, I knew I would have to continue to whore the same. However, I hoped to receive a sort of help. On the contrary, I had only a bunch of blows. When I came back from work, he got my money I had earned and he used it to drink, to smoke, to play, to spread it with other women. It was not good. I decided to leave him. But I need a strategy. He would have never easily given up to his comfortable source of earning, without working and without taxes. I had to let him meet a friend of mine, a quite silly girl I had met on the street. It was just this strategy, which let me leave him and she was the unconscious means.

Then I made part of an organized group: we worked a lot: swindles, frauds, robberies, extortions. We were able to get money from old sucker people, ingenuous housewives, and ignorant workers. The leader was Romeo, a boy coming from Gaeta or Formia, who had bright ideas, even if some of them were too much adventurous. He had studied for a month to organize a plan: we had to get a T.I.R., full of razor blade. We got it, but then something went wrong and they caught almost everyone. Only him got off scot-free (got away with it). They condemned me, giving me two years and six months of prisons, but I did not expiate all the period, because I had no other criminal punishments. When I went out, I wound up my feet that beast of Anacleto, who wanted me back to him. But this time I became clever and I established some conditions. Luckily, they killed him while we were in negotiations, for a drug order bad cropped he had dumped to someone not very willing to be subjected to scams.

Nun Leonilde got a job in a fruit job for me. She was a good Nun, who had taken care of my family since I was a child. She tried to help us, finding supports, medicines, used cloths, leading us to the right way, without any results, of course. She had a particular affection for me. She had always loved me. In that shop, I had been working for four months. The wage was good and sometimes the owner gave me some fruits, vegetables, and something else, but it was very little. One Saturday evening caught the right moment and I took away the daily earning. That shop was full of customers, a flowing of coming in and out. The owner was rich, so, what was wrong with keeping something for me? He did not denounce me only because he wanted to stay far from justice.

Nun Leonilde, besides, got very angry and she did not want to have anything to do with me, anymore. She said I was ungrateful, deplorable and I deserved to be left to my destiny, which was already signed, after all.

In Prison, of course, in prison and just here I have been, over and over again. People said I am immoral, but I do not know what moral means, nobody had never taught me to distinguish between good and evil: I have been taught only to fight to survive. As a child, I saw my mother having sex with repulsive and rude men; I saw my father making every kind of crimes, teaching my brother and I, how to rub, to steal and to cheat. I could

71

see my brothers pretending to be crippled to cheat people and I did the same.

All seemed normal to me; it was our job, by which we had earned our food. I have never known any other possible way to live. When I found that way, it was too late, I had already become a cockroach and I could not turn myself into a dragonfly; that was my way of living. When I robbed a little old woman, who had offered me a little money, because I told her I was hungry, it did not seem to me such a big crime. I robbed her fur coat, her beg and a golden bracelet. She was a rich old lady, and I am sure that robbery had not been a big damage for her. I know, she was in the hospital for shock, but I could not know she would have been so frightened. Anyway, I had given her only a couple of punches. Moreover, why should an old lady have a fur coat and a young girl like me has no decent dress? It was an injustice! During the trial, they told me I was a criminal, lacking of sense of humanity. I don't think so. I suffer when other people suffer. I felt so sorry when I saw Cristina crying desperate because we had stolen her car. It was a new Fiat Panda: she had bought it by a monthly payment, making many sacrifices. I gave it her back. Of course, I asked her two thousand lyres in turn, because I could not give it back free, what would the band have thought about me? And more, even if Cristina was not a rich girl, she had been a lucky girl, more than me. She had her parents, who took care of her and a boyfriend who loved her.

I have never been loved. My husband is not really bad, but he does not love me, at all. He only loves wine, bear and whisky; and as soon as he drinks, he becomes aggressive and violent. This scar on my forehead is the result of one of his last benders. It was 3 o'clock a.m. and I had just come back home from work. Tired and sleepy, I went into the bathroom and I found him inside the bathtub. I tried to get him out of there and put him on the bed but he was sleeping as a millstone. I had already decided to leave him there for the rest of the night when he suddenly woke up. Stunned by the alcohol he flung on my forehead a pottery soap dish, which was handily. Few days later, I had my revenge. While he was sleeping peacefully drunk as usual near me, I throw him down by a kick. he made a terrible noise. I thought he had his head broken; on the contrary, he continued to sleep on the floor as if nothing had happened. The day after, he suffered for his headache. What can I hope with such a husband? When we got married, he was a body shop mechanic and he was also good at making it. He used to drink even in that period, but I was sure I could make him stop drinking. Besides, he had been getting worse and now it is late, he is an alcoholic, addicted to alcohol, as it is said nowadays.

Many times, I wondered how could have been my life if I had been born in another family, in another environment, in another city but there is no answer to this question. Maybe, I would have been a singer: I have always had a nice voice and a nice appearance, or a housewife, with husband and children, who barely made ends meet, as my friend Pina. She is a childhood friends of mine, who was part of the band of little evils, too. However, she had married with a painter when she was eighteen, a good man, who is paid daily wages and he earns when he works. They live in Vicaria suburb in a slum, and they have got three beautiful children. She spends all the time washing, cooking, ironing, darning and she is always tired and nervous. At the beginning, I did not think she had made the right choice, marrying her painter. She lived with difficulty, with sacrifices and anxiety: I did not envy her. On the contrary, now I can see she has expectations, which comes from her children's plans. For her children, she had spent all her energies, she has placed all her hopes on them. The children had grown up and they are going to get their diplomas, they have engaged and she has been living waiting for their placements.

Besides, I have no children. I have nobody to put my hopes on, I have no plans, no expectations, I feel useless, and there is nobody who can refill this sense of emptiness I have inside, which is more and more growing by passing of time." Teresa went out of prison few months later. I saw her again at the front door, waiting for her visiting to her prisoned sister. "You know, I get my head together I have found a job." she said. "Nice to know that. And what type of job?" I asked her. "I have put a desk on Domiziana (a well-known road in Campania (TN.) I sell smuggled cigarettes".

Caserta, 1993.

ANNA

Anna is not young nor beautiful, but her energy makes her nice and talkative. Fair eyes, direct gaze, she seems to know well life and its dramas. She spontaneously gives advice and her personal opinions to everybody, even when they are not requested. "People think that prison is a static place, where everyone is closed inside her cell, all day long, without doing nothing, looking at the roof, but it is not so. In prison passions fire up; there are new dynamics, external logic stories are reflected inside the prison, too. It is a completely different world: a forced cohabitation, of course, a limited freedom, rigid rules that gives birth to intolerance and inconveniences. You know, I understand your job is hard, for its responsibility. You have to think too many things, to plan, to organize, to get in touch to every kind of people or way of thinking. I can understand your job because in the past I made the same: you know, I was a director of a house, a house, well to better saying, a house for prostitution. It was clandestine, of course. However, I was always in anxiety for food, diseases, and customers, for everything. You never know what can happen. However, I wanted to talk about the fighting between Fatima and Amina; they have given each other a good hiding. Have you seen how they are seriously reduced very badly? Above all Amina. Besides, I can say those people are pacific, joyful, Nigerians, Senegalese, Zairian, from Ghana, they are good, nice people, but they are also easily inflaming, they are emotional, passionate, they are not able to control their own reactions. Sometimes, they build up endless quarrels for useless reasons. I call them "equatorial quarrels".

There are a lot of them here inside, but I can stop them. I know well African people, because my husband was Nigerian. Do you want to know why they have quarrelled? As you know, living in the same cell, they make shopping in common, dividing their money. Therefore, Fatima was angry because Amine usually has many showers, using too much soap bath. Besides, we need to save money, because there is not enough. However, we have to understand her, poor woman. After being suffering thirsty in her country, where dryness prevents the growing of grass and the desert overwhelms villages around, it seems unbelievable to her to see such a plenty of water here, hearing it flowing warm and generous on her face, body and on her hair. They are just like that: passionate people, sometimes they become fierce. As a matter of the fact, they are people always in war. Have you seen what happened in Ruanda last year? Hutu have killed Tutsi community. There have been terrible things over there. Men, women and children had been reduced in pieces, alive, with machete. Hundreds of thousands of victims. In addition, they are all Catholics! Of course, nobody loose the opportunity to consider them savage, as if some things like these, could only come from Africa. However, what about Stalin and Hitler? Were they savage, too? The truth is that human being is naturally violent in any latitude and longitude, and in any type of society. He is ready to show his worst aspects to make his interests prevail or reach power. Woe betide if you are fragile, or show your vulnerability: immediately someone comes up to use you trampling on, prevailing you, humiliating you, and exploiting the situation at his advantage. The world is a grip, which grinds you as soon as it finds your weak spots. I know it well, because I have spent all my life fighting for preventing others to crush me.

My existence has not been so easy. I was born in Terracina, in a slum, in the suburb of the city, in an unlucky family. My father, alcoholic and unemployed, has always done nothing but beating his wife and children. My mother was a kind of human wreck, who endured everything without complaining, without any reaction, nor defending her children. I remember her always with the same dirty and worn rags on, disordered hair and with her eternal contracted, tired and suffering face. She cleaned the block of flats, the offices, shops; she started early in the morning and went on all the daylong. She worked hard but money was never enough at home, even because most of it finished in my father's hands, who spent it in wine or beer, cigarettes or women. We were three children, grown up without rules, nor love and education, abandoned to ourselves. My two eldest brothers were authentic thugs. They began very early rubbing cars, bag snatching, stealing and ransacking. They came in and out the prison, as if it was their home.

Besides, I was different. I was meditative and responsible, even if they were useless qualities in that context. At the age of ten, I had all the house duties on my shoulders; I had to cook, to do the laundry, to make the house cleaning. At my father's coming back home from work, if I did not cook the lunch, he dealt me a bunch of blows. I was a sad little girl, very unhappy and alone. I had no friends, because I had left school and I spent all my time at home as a prison. Sometimes I looked out of the window, gazing the outdoor world, which it seemed to me out of reach, far from my misery existence. When I think about that period of my life, I feel very sad. Here inside the prison, I feel better, because I have some friends to speak with. I had felt a great envy for a little girl, who I saw passing with her mum in front of my house every morning. She had a red coat, varnished shoes and a book bag. I know her name was Elisa, because I have heard her being called by her mum…"Elisa…Elisa". She was always sulky, maybe because she did not want to go to school, as besides I wished, in spite of staying at home, washing and cooking. I envied her, above all for that read coat. I still remember her even after many years and maybe she ignores my existence.

At the age of fourteen, I was a little woman, already shaped. One mourning my father came back home drunk as usual. He had a dopey expression on his face; his gaze was foggy and moved as a robot. Stumbling he propped against furniture and walls, avoiding to fall down. He released a disgusting smell of tobacco and wine. I was not surprised of it. It was not the first time I saw him in that condition. I considered him as a useless man; since I was born, he had told me only few words and none of affection. He left himself dropped on the bed, without saying a word. Our house was desert, my mother was at work and my brothers were around, making disasters. I came into the room to put cleaned cloths into the chest of drawers, when suddenly he got up of the bed stumbling; I tried to raise him up, thinking he had a sudden illness, but all at once, he grasped me strongly and throw me on the bed. I tried to get up away upset, but he pushed me back and jumped on me. He strongly squashed me with his massive body, until I was breathless. My upset soon became fear; I was in a complete state of anxiety. I felt as I was falling down into an abyss without bottom. With a hand he rose up my skirt, tearing up my underwear; meanwhile, by the other hand, he closed up my mouth until I was breathless. I tried to react with all my strength, ticking and punching him, but I soon realized to be completely unable, powerless. He stopped my arms keeping my wrists tightly as in a grip, reducing me motionless. I felt his heavy and gasping breath, while my painful and desperate crying was lost in the empty house.

A nightmare, I had lived a nightmare from which I have never waken up. Was it possible what was happening to me? I cried, I prayed, but with no result. It was a terrible and traumatic experience. For many years, I have been unable to remember it, nor to speak about it. I had completely removed it. Then, after my father's death, little by little, I picked up it from my subconscious. Thinking back on it, I have thrills of horror and disgust. I would not remember it at all. I spent my next days closed into the bathroom, crying without eating nor sleeping, wishing only not to see anybody, while everyone around me were acting as always, ignoring me.

It is difficult to explain what I feel after such a kind of experience. You feel an oppressive sense of shame, disgust, emptiness; you grow up an incomprehensible sense of guilty; you seem to be useless, hiding the fact, telling nothing to anyone, pushing it back, bluffing, as nothing had never happened. However, sufferance is always behind the corner and it is ready to jump up at the first negative experience of your life. After some days, I needed to ask help to someone, and I did it with the only one person who could surely help me: my mother.

I tried to tell her, to let her understand something, whishing she could react against her husband anyway. On the contrary, she looked at me as an idiot, mumbling some words about misfortune of being a woman and on the spirit of resignation I should have. I did not understand anything, but I realized she did not care anything about me and about what had happened to me. At the beginning I felt the gravity of that fact only on emotional point of view; only after time I realized its huge significance. I think that my father was so much drunk he did not understand what he was doing. Anyway, I have been hated him for all my life and even more I have been hated my mother for her cowardice and laziness.

It is terrible hating your own parents. You lost your roots, your reference points, but I could not avoid it. After that speech with my mother, I suddenly changed my behaviour: I became rebel, because of my destiny and intolerant towards everyone around me. I was no more available to endure others' moral misery. At that point, I decided. I was fed up with that cage of fouls and I ran away. Maybe it is better to say that I went away without greeting anyone. No one came and found me and I had never come back to them. I went to Rome, to a far relative of us, who sometimes had used to visit us. I had found her address in a letter she had sent us time before. She did not received me with happiness, but she received me. I was grateful she did not go into deep about the reason of my running away from home. She made some questions, but when she saw my reticence, she asked no more. "Your Family is very singular," she said. "Your father is a lowlife, your mother is a miserable, and your brothers are irresponsible. I hope you can save yourself". I stayed with her for a short time, then, I went to live in a rent room, in a miserable slum of the city.

I made every kind of work to survive: I was a skivvy in a restaurant, a servant in a public toilet, a waitress in a hotel and then I met a typical man who put me on the street. It is useless to tell it now; the screenplay is always the same. He pursued me with a false kindness, he gave me little presents, which I considered special ones and he won me over. He was the first person, who gave me some kind of attention, but it was an interested attention; as a matter of the fact soon after a while, he throw me on the street. I had a good amount of customers, because I was very young but he got all my earns. I could not react because he was a criminal, violent and without qualms, he scared me, he could easily vanished me, since nobody would have looked for me. Fortunately, after two years, he was arrested for rubbery and he spent few time in prison. When he went out he never looked for me. I moved to another city: Reggio Emilia. I went on as a whore but at least I earned on my own. I rented a little house, very humble with broken windows and spots of moisture everywhere. I caught customers and I brought them there.

Being a whore is not easy. It is an exhausting stressful work: you never know who you can meet: maniacs, crooks, thieves, but I have always succeeded. What I cannot afford is solitude. An imposed solitude. If you do this job, you cannot trust in anybody. Women are envious and always in competition, men are dangerous and always ready to exploit you. Friendship does not exist and even love is rare. It is a cynic and cruel environment.

I had never had a true love, since I met Gani. It was the period called "giorni della merla", the coolest last days of the wintertime. A carpet of snow covered the whole city and a cutting frozen wind blew until the bones. He stopped me in the street, wearing a short mock-leather jacket, which surely could not save him from freezing. He spoke English and I spoke Italian, anyway we understood the same. He was looking for the seat

81

of Caritas, maybe the public canteen. He had a sculptured body, an awesome smile, brightening teeth, contrasting with his ebony skin. I have never been racist. In my opinion, man could be judged only for his heart, not for the colour of his skin. I gazed him and I was flashed. Love at first sight. "I am the Caritas". I answered him, laughing. I brought him at home, which was not very nice, but it was a shelter. I cooked him rice and scrambled eggs. I have always been good at cooking. I did not tell him about my real job. I thought it was not the case. I lied: I told him I was looking for a new job because I had just lost that of waitress at the bar.

Therefore, it started a long and happy period of my life. He was joyful, sweet, kind. He gave me his time and attention. He treated me as no one had done before, with love. Even if he was younger, he made me feel beautiful and attractive. Of course, he had some surge of anger, but it lasted for short and I forgave him everything. We could only merry by religious rite, because he was clandestine. Fortunately, he was catholic. Father Daniele, a Franciscan missionary we had met at Caritas, celebrated the marriage and soon he became our spiritual father. At the ceremony, there were only some of his fellow's citizens and a young couple of Senegalese, who we were meeting in that period. I wore a wonderful dress, light blue silk, which had cost me a lot. I have always dreamt the bridal gown and a white voile; I was almost tempted to buy one, but to say the truth I thought it was not the case.

It was like living a fair: we were full of wishes and plans. He set up a stall of ethnic jewelleries and things, with which he went around for local fairs. I found a job as a servant in a private school of nuns, thanks to father Daniele's help. I worked a lot and at the end of lessons, I had to clean the classrooms, the toilets and other locals of the school. When I came back home I cooked dinner and I worked at home: I cleaned, removing dust, I ironed. That life was very hard for me, but I faced everything with joy, even if we had little money. He was used to poverty, to hardness, to sacrifices; it seemed that nothing was heavy for him. I taught him Italian language and I learnt some words of Ibo, his mother tongue. He told me many things about his country, a problematic land, unhealthy, which, even if it is plenty of sources, it has a poor population, because of the exploitation made by mighty people. Homesick, he used to speak about his childhood, spent in a village near Enugu, the most important city of the country. He remembered the mangrove plants of the tropical forest, the fried cakes made up of manioc flour, which his grandma used to cook, the dance and the rhythm of the parties. He described his home, his family, his people, poor but respectable. His mother was very beautiful, he said, dressing in typical multi-coloured clothes of that place, with wooden and chord ornament; a sweet and smiling woman, even if she worked hard in cotton plantation for few money. "Living in Europe is a fortune", he said, "you are lucky and you don't know it, the compulsory and free education, the medical assistance for everyone, the retirements for seniors are things which we cannot imagine. The wellness in which you live is a daydream, which let us leave our country to come here. The western world is so rich, that it can help unlucky populations, but its selfishness let it ignore the tragedy of a continent which is dying for hungry under the eyes of whom is too stuffed". He thought about his father, who for all his life, had been working in a coal mine, dark, oppressive and dangerous. He compared him with Italian workers, defended or protected by laws, insurance, medical assistance. He told me about the sufferance of his fellows, during the Independence war in Biafra. The federal government put the country under siege, interrupted food provisions and all the population was grinded into a grip of hungry. The cruel armed force made the rest. Hundreds of thousands people died. He was fourteen. He lost almost all his family: two younger sisters and his mother. His sisters had been wasted away day by day, reduced as skeletons, with their swollen belly and their wrinkled skin, as many other Biafra children showed in magazines all over the indifferent world. Before her death, his mother let him promise to run away from Africa. "This is a miserable, fierce land, with eternal wars." –she said. - "You can never live in peace nor in wealthy here. It is a desperate continent. Go to Europe and try to conquer a better life for you and for your children."

It had taken many year to come here. His friend, a police officer, had found him a link with a criminal trafficker organization, which let him get documents and visas in turn of a huge amount of money; he had already been paying with a high rate of interests. In spite of the memory of all those miseries, homesick of his land was very strong, even if he had many Nigerians friends with whom he could feel as at home. "The emigrants has no more their homelands"- He told me- "I am a stranger here, it would be the same in Africa. Here I miss my land, I miss Africa, and once in Africa I would miss what I have here."

It had been three wonderful years. He had filled up my life. Everything I could do was only for him, and in the evening, I came back home happy, thinking about meeting him again. By the passing of time, he developed his business, African handmade scarfs, bags and necklaces, which found a great demand. We started hoping to realize something, in spite of working only to survive. We could change home, buy a new car, maybe used but in good conditions, instead of that beat-up car he used to go from a fair to another. However, expenses were too many. A part from the monthly payment for his debt, we had also to pay a bride to the criminal organization for the illegal stall at the market.

A proverb says: the good is peaceful until the evil wants. And the evil, to better saying, the evils arrived soon. They were represented by the criminals, the Nigerians traffickers, greed and cruel. They had known about our wellness and they decided to double the bride. They asked a huge amount, impossible to pay for us. Rami came back home very angry and desperate. I soon realized the dangerous situation in which he was. I tried to be careful; they came back many times, threatening him of payback if he had not paid the debt, without listening to his reasons. I was not calm at all. I spent my nights in anxiety. We had to give up that business and change it with another one, but he did not agree. He said that if we endure every time, we would be overwhelmed in any case. They would never accept our choice to change our business activity. They used to control the other extra communitarian work.

I thought to get back to my old job, prostitution, but it was not so easy. I would have been again in that context and take again contacts in a world I have chosen to give up. It would take too much time. After that day, we were continually quarrelling. I am afraid I had never hidden it. One evening, on my name day, I cooked "parmigiana di melanzane" (T.N.: A typical Italian dish with aubergines) he liked very much. I laid the table carefully, I opened a bottle of wine I had bought in the evening and I waited for him. I waited without results because he had never come back. I had been waiting for him all the night. Early in the morning, I started my researches. I looked everywhere, at his friends' home, at the fair places where he used to go, asking for him to every coloured people of the city, to every market seller who had met him, but nobody had seen him or met him.

My desperation was growing by passing of time. Father Daniele tried to find him too. He got in touch with all Caritas seat of the nearest places, with the Hospitals, with homeless, borderlines or addicted people and even with the Nigerian Embassy. His friends begun to look for him everywhere in the city, without results. At the end, I decided to ask to the police, but it was useless, he disappeared, vanished in the air. I had been looking for him desperately for a whole year, spreading his photos among the people he had met him, I put advertises on local newspapers. If there had been the TV program "Who saw him?" (A famous Italian TV reportage program about missing people) I would have called for their help. Among his letters, I found his house address in Africa. There was only his old father. I wrote him with the help of a friend. He answered he had no news. I had suffered a lot. Even now, after many years if I think of him and our special love, I cannot stop crying. His memory brings me back to such a big sorrow, which had never found peace. I often regret not having told him about my life. He was sympathetic. He would have understood me, but I was so scared to lose him. I regret a baby: he would be a special one, or maybe a little girl, with blue eyes as mine and black skin or fair curly hair. He or she would have been a nice baby. It had to go in this way and I had to end my life as I started: alone.

Arienzo, 1995.

SAMIRA

When she came to prison, as soon as she was arrested, she was in a crisis of anxiety and she gave savage shouts against everyone was trying to come close to her. She seemed confused, scared and in a clear state of shock. They brought her in infirmary where they gave her a sedative. After few days, she seemed to be calm, but as desperate as before. She asked to speak with me. When she came into my office, I looked at her carefully.

She was twenty, no more. Her skin was very dark, and her physical appearance gave clear evidence of her Nigerian provenience. Her beauty, which in origin had to be considerable, was completely marred by a big scar, which cut through her left side of the face. Her Italian was clearly comprehensible, but her voice was often broken by sobs and moans of crying.

"I could not understand the reason of my arrest. I was sleeping in my friend's house when suddenly police came in and arrested everyone. I have been here in Italy for two years and it has been two years that I have not seen my mother and all my family.

During this period, everything had happened to me. I could experience the atrocity which human beings are able to do. Now, the only thing I wish is coming back home, to my country.

I was born in Benin City, an important centre in Nigeria and there I had spent my childhood and my youth. At that time, I could not imagine that life is so cruel. I lived in the peaceful atmosphere of my family. That was my world, for me. I did not know what violence, abuse of power or hungry were. My grandma was a special woman. My parents went to work and she used to keep the house tidy, she washed, cooked, tied up. Even if she was not young, she had a great energy; she had been my reference point during my childhood. I can still remember her fairy tales, full of mystery and magic she used to tell me and to help me sleeping sooner, while, as a little, innocent child, I listened to her astonished, happily crouched in her protective arms. She was very tied with her land traditions and she regretted our people denied our ancient cultural identity.

My father worked as a nurse in the civic hospital and my mother had a grocery shop. We were not rich, but we went on with dignity. My brothers attended the primary school and I attended the high school. I had a boyfriend. His name was Adel. All my friends envied me. His wonderful, velvety, intelligent and joyful eyes gave a particular light. He was a year older and he was the best at school. He dreamt to become an aeronautic engineer and working in USA or in England, after his graduation. His plans seemed to be unreal but I admired him. He had a strong willing and he will have success, surely.

The tragedy blow up when I was fifteen. My father was killed in a shop during a robbery. Criminals shot him, right to his head. He had come in to buy some light bulbs. In my country, robberies were normal. Misery, frustration, angry, together with the lack of ideals and morality, create cruel and rude feelings among new generations. Our life was completely upset from that moment. To the sorrow for our father's death, we added the worrying for our future, due to the economic uncertainty of my whole family.

In that period, Adel was closer to me, but then, as often happens, everyone took his own path. He went on with his life and I had to stop my studies. Without a stable monthly wage, we were in economic difficulty. My mother's little shop did not give back enough, moreover our suppliers, acknowledged about our financial situation, started to ask for their credits, without any discount, while our customers, who used to buy for credit, did not solve their payments in time or at all. We were forced to close. My mother and I were the only members of the family able to work. She found a job as a servant in a house for old people, for a low wage. I worked for a delivery company, but it soon failed and I became unemployed. We were in great financial crisis and we could not afford to the needs of five people. Often, at night in the dark I could hear my mother crying while the others were sleeping.

I was eighteen when a friend told me to work in Europe. "You can earn a lot, there." - He said- "within few years you can collect a little fortune, come back home and live without any problem." My mother was doubtfully and my grandma strongly contrary. She thought I was too young to go alone to a foreign country, to a world full of dangers and mysteries. On the contrary, I was enthusiastic. This proposal satisfied my spirit of adventure and my desire to get in touch with a new, rich and different reality.

Two persons came and visited us. They offered us a job as caregiver to seniors, in a comfortable family in Italy. They showed me an agreement by which I assumed the duty to give back to the organization a large amount of money within three years, for the traveling expenses and for the needed documents procedures. It seemed too much money. I was not used to those numbers. When they noticed my doubts, they granted me huge earns which would make me able to give all back within less than three years.

They were smooth- tongued and able sellers. It is the ghost of misery responsible of irreparable mistakes. When I went away, my mother, my grandma were crying, while my little brothers were celebrating me. I was going to leave my country, my home, my family to face with a jungle overrun by beasts. I had prepared my luggage carefully, my linen and casual clothes, which my grandma made for me.

At the departure, I wore the best clothes, to give the best impression to my employers. We travelled at night. In addition, we arrived in Lagos at the first lights at sunrise. A woman took me together with other girls, recruited for the same purpose. It was in that context that I met Wilma. She came from a village near the Capital. She was very beautiful but fragile and sensitive. She often cried and the unknown terrified her. She was seventeen and she had never left her little suburb. She told me she was travelling to help her family, who lived in poverty. She had five brothers and her father, who was very ill, could not find a job. I saw her scared and undefended. I started to give her protection.

We were entrusted with a woman, called Betty, a gross and massive woman, too much striking and showy make up on her face. She kindly behaved but I could perceive a false behaviour, on the contrary. After superficial controls and short procedures fulfilment at the airport of Lagos, we went to Italy. It was the first time I travelled by plane. I looked at the abyss under me through out the window and I could see my land going far away. I felt a strange sense of anxiety and detachment. We landed in Milan; Malpensa airport was wonderful; it showed me a new opulent world, which I could only glimpse on magazine, photos, TV or simply imagined through someone's descriptions. I would have seen shop-windows, bars, places, but it was impossible. Betty was in a hurry. The city was in such a deep fog, as it seemed solid. Around there were milky beams of light and narrow fleeting shadows, big and fast cars were splashing drops of mug on us. A cold and cutting atmosphere covered me as in a freezing coat. My outfit was not appropriate for that unusual climate and I shivered in front of that unknown scene. We went on by train until Turin.

A shady man came with us. He was scaring at a simply sight. He was Betty's boyfriend. His name was Dani. He had long and thick sideburn climbing down his chin and an opened silk skirt on his hairy breast, which showed a big golden necklace. During the travel, I began to realize that it was not as I had thought and my grandma was right. However, I went on reassuring Wilma, aware of the fact that if I had showed my doubts, I would have frightened her very much. When we arrived in Turin, they set us in a big flat. It was as I had always imagined an Italian flat should be: well refined, big, with three bedrooms and two bathrooms, covered by ceramic tiles. It was quite empty, with essential old furniture, but, in dining room, there was a nice squared table in the centre of the room, with a glass cover upon it.

At that point, Betty's behaviour completely changed. She became rude and aggressive, showing all her perverse nature. Together with Dani, without any useless words, she clearly told us we would chase an illusion, because nobody in Italy would have employed African clandestine for legal jobs. So, we had no choice, we had to accept to become whores, trying to get the best profit at least, until the complete payment of the amount of money we had agreed to give back for travelling expenses.

91

They threatened us, revenging against our families in Nigeria, whereas we would have refused to do tit. The organization was well extended and full of clutches. At that statement, I felt to collapse deep into a desperate abyss. Alone, in a foreign country, without speaking the language and without any help, how could I escape far from that situation? I was scared, but I said nothing. I realized I was not in condition to rebel against it. I thought to take time to decide what to do. The other girls, too, did not say a world, but at a deeper sight, some of them were not surprised nor frightened. I had a clear idea that they knew which our destiny was. Of course, I could not expect their help, nor their will to react.

Besides, Wilma had an endless crisis of hysteria, she became to weep, cry, and thrash about. Betty and Dani tried to keep her clam by promises and threats but they failed. All at once, she got closer to the door, as she was running away. At that point, with a shocking cruelty, they began to beat her up by kicks and punches, covering her with offenses and insults, under the astonished eyes of all of us. I could see her upset by sobs and blows, I would have helped her, but I was not brave enough. I will be bringing inside of me the memory of those terrible moments for all my life. Suddenly, I saw her falling down. The strong hits she had received bumping violently her head against the corner of the glassy table and standing motionless on the floor, covered by bruisers and blood. We put her on the bed and we tried to reanimate her. Her deathly pale scared every one of us. She gave feeble breath, barely detectable. The two, worried and scared, called a doctor, who came after an hour. He had white skin; he was young, with ambiguous appearance. He visited her and shaking his head, he showed all his powerless. I did not understand what he said but I think

92

he had advised a recover in the hospital. When the doctor went away, Betty and Dani began to quarrel. They had discussed for long time on what they had to do, analysing each detail, but Wilma was still in her bed. I had been watching over her all the night, while in the house there was an atmosphere of anxiety and fear. They exchanged blames on each other. I did not know what to do. Sometimes I watered her front head and I made her smell some perfume, as I had seen doing in my country when you want to bring someone back to life. I checked her breath, I called her, hoping she would wake up from that stated come, but nothing happened. At sunrise, her front head was frozen and that weak breath was vanished at all.

Dani dragged her body into the car and brought it away, only God knows where. I thought to her parents, who would have never seen her nor would they have known what happened to their daughter, they had left alone to go in search of fortune.

That was my first day in Italy. I was grasped by the net of a cruel criminal organization, people without any care, ready to do everything to get earns and benefits from other misery and unhappiness. The facts had terrified me. I realized I had no chance and I went into the street, becoming a whore.

At the beginning, it was terrible. It was February: the air was freezing and the city was covered by fog. We all were forced to dress with short and light low- necked clothes. I crumbled for fear and freeze. Doing this job, I have met every kind of people: maniacs, criminals, violent, even someone polite, but they were rare. I earned a lot, but all my money ended in the hand of Betty, who, when she was unsatisfied, began to humiliate with every type of oppression and dealt me a bunch of blows, leaving me fasted. It was a hellish life.

In that period, I met Fausto, a young man, not handsome, but sensitive and good. He was a worker in a chemical Industry and during his free time, he used to come and visit me. I did not know he was married. I have never asked him directly and he had been always very vague. However, I did not care about it. I spent with him my unique peaceful moments I had had in that period. When I could escape from Danni's control, we went around the city by his old economy car and we went sometime to eat in some of the cheap restaurant in the centre of the city. One time, he brought me to the cinema, watching a beautiful movie I liked very much. He had been touched by my sad story, he would help me in order that I could denounce the criminal facts made by my exploiters, but I did not want: after Wilma's death, I was terrified by Betty's threats. At Christmas Fausto gave me a clock, a cheap thing, but I thought it was a wonderful present. I did not show it to anybody and I kept it jealously hidden, fearing someone could take it away. He brought me in the streets of the centre where mostly you can feel the magic atmosphere of Christmas. I like to see the joyful air, crowd everywhere, the adorned shop windows and the lights in the streets and all those people who came out of shops, charged of bags and boxes.

One morning, getting up early I felt a strange illness: vertigos, nausea, and gagging. I set discouraged and sadden, wandering what was happening. It did not take so much time to understand I was pregnant. I was imprudent when I told it to a friend of mine, who immediately reported all to Betty. Together with Danni, she soon faced me: They wanted I made abortion, but I refused. I did not want to get away the little being who was growing inside me. They tried to convince me, at first using hypocrite manners and believable reasons, then, when they saw my determination, they became aggressive, beating me violently, wildly, as they had done with Wilma. I tried to defend myself with all my strength, reacting as a wounded beast. All at once, I found a bottle and I grasped it from my back. When I tried to hit Danni, he got out a knife and he injured my face. I felt a stabbing on my cheek. I saw my clothes and floor red stained, while my blood was flowing on my neck and on my hands. The dread and pain fogged up my mind. I fell down as a dead and I fainted.

When I woke up, there was the same doctor who was suturing my wound. He asked me something in English but I did not answer. He answered me again, but my silence continued. I was shocked, with my eyes fixed on the roof, my body motionless, my face pale and without any expression. I had been in this way for long. I was like a robot, with swallow expression and my gaze lost in emptiness.

Days went on, my conditions did not get better and Betty realized that her source of earning had been draining. My pregnancy, my physical and psychological illness, my cut on my cheek had created a disadvantageous situation for a no more lucrative exploitation. They needed to get rid of me, it was better to sell me to another pimp, Wanda: that was her name.

She came soon and took me in Naples. We travelled by car all the day and we arrived late in the evening. The darkness had already dropped on the city and I did not see very much but I soon noticed a different atmosphere: warmer and less hostile than that in Turin. The flat was on ground floor. Each room had gates at windows, except the bathroom, which overlooked a little courtyard on the back. It was quite a humble house, placed in a street with a lot of traffic, near the railway and it hosted other girls. They came from different countries. They were suspicious, aggressive and pugnacious, that's why I could not become their friend. Wanda was forty and even if she was an exploiting snake, she looked like less cunning than Betty. She set me in a room alone. She took care of me, to let me recover and she patiently waited for my healing. Soon after, she sent me on the street. My pregnancy seemed not a problem for her. On the contrary, she did not deny me food, keeping me relaxed, when I had not to work, of course. Her boyfriend was always there, but he spoke few words.

In Naples, I had some problems: customers refused me, because of my scar, moreover because I was pregnant. My pregnancy gave me a lot of disturbs: vomits, tiredness, headache, but I still worked on the street. Every day, late in the afternoon, they brought us to the extreme suburb of the town, in a sleazy and run- down neighbourhood, toxic by traffic and smog. I was exhausted by stress, working annoyance and worrying for childbirth. I was homesick of Fausto and I often used to call him. I knew I could get nothing by that relationship. He belonged to another world. However, he represented an anchor to grasp. Surely, he was the father of my baby because I had no protected sexual intercourses only with him. He had promised many times to reach me in Naples but that had never happened. To say the truth, I was not afraid, because I did not want he saw my scarred face.

Motherhood was my only hope.

That baby represented the aim of my fight to survive, even if I could not imagine how it would take place in my existence. Wanda let me do an ultrasound exam so I could know it was a boy and I decided to call him

96

Amdi, as my father. I would take care of him every day, but at night, when I had to work who would have taken care of him. Wanda reassured me, smiling: "Don't worry, my dear. All will be ok, when that moment comes." I bought some cloths for him, but not a cradle yet. The pregnancy months had spent in that way. The days before the childbirth I concentrated my thoughts on that event.

Contractions came at the end of August, at sunrise. Immediately Wanda called an obstetrician, who came soon after. My labour did not last very much and the childbirth happened without any difficulties. The baby was wonderful, with white skin and dark hair. I saw him only for a while. Soon after that, they gave me something, which made me fall asleep. When I woke up, it was maybe midday and the sun came deep inside the room, bringing an intolerable heating. I was tired, confused, and drippy of sweat and I felt a strange feeling of anxiety. I called Wanda asking her about my baby, but she answered with many inane excuses.

Many hours had passed. Night came down and in the house. There was a deep silence. I was nervous and impatient, I had not seen my baby yet and this fact worried me a lot. All at once, I realized I had not heard his crying for all day, and I was overwhelmed by a terrible suspicion. Even if I was weak and suffering, I could get up of my bed while everyone was sleeping. I looked for him everywhere in the house, but he was not here. I made Wanda awaked and with angry I asked her where she had brought him. "He is not here, no more!" she answered. "We had given him to people who can raise him up better than you. Forget him! You could not give him time nor the needed care." A bow in my stomach would have caused me less pain. I was upset. Where could my little baby be? A poor little being was overwhelmed by human cruelty. Wanda had sold him as an object with fierce indifference.

It was still night when I collected my few things. I climbed over the window of the bath. I ran away from that house. I could not stay there more than a while. I walked without a target. The street was desert. Some cars ran fast, while my shadow was getting longer on the pavement under the light of lampposts. When I arrived at the railway, the waiting room was close. Some homeless were sleeping on benches; I set down on a stone chair. I was upset by contraction of my belly. I had loss of blood and shivers. Looking around me, I saw nobody who could help me and without realizing it, I fell down, losing my senses.

I woke up in a hospital. I had headache, a needle put in my arm for blood transfusion and a drip feed in the other one. A weak beam of light came through the closed roller shutter. I did not know if it was day or night. I had been motionless for long time, looking around. There was nobody in. In half-light, I could see a little bared place: a little table, a chair, a nightstand. I rang the bell and a nurse came in, followed by a doctor. He was old, and behaved as a father. He gauged my wrist, measured my blood pressure, listened to my heartbeats, controlled my temperature and after that, he said: "Madam, You have had a bleeding, you lost too much blood. Fortunately, we stopped it. "Then he added: "You surely have recently had a childbirth, would you like to tell me what happened? Where is the baby?" It was the first time that someone called me "Madam". I gazed him astonished but I said no words. I did not know what to tell him. I closed my eyes and I stayed silently. "Tell me at least, where are you from"- he continued- "Maybe from Nigeria?" I answered with a gesture of approval. "From what place exactly?"- He insisted on- "Benin City" I whispered.

Few hours later two women came in. One of them wore a police uniform and she was quite young. The other was a Nigerian who spoke Italian, English and my language, too. They asked me my name, age, my residence; visa, my marital status, my address and then they asked me about my baby again. I realized I could not avoid the question anymore. I had to say something to the police. Therefore, without considering the risk I could have, I decided to tell everything to them, about Betty and Wanda, about humiliations I had to suffer for childbirth and the baby. I felt a mix of sorrow, angry, regret and at the same time, I felt the need to share my suffering with someone. When I was alone soon after, touching my face, I felt the rigid scar left by Danni and immediately I realized they would have arrested Betty, Wanda and the others and I should have testify against them. I was again in panic: those cruel people would have never forgive me. I tossed and turned into my bed, consumed by anxiety and confused by both a strong desire of Justice and the fear to suffer again those criminals' revenge. Therefore, the day after, before the police woman came back to finish my confession, I ran away, avoiding the staff's control.

For many days, I had slept wherever I found a place and I ate whatever I found to eat. I had to hide myself to escape from those criminals who were surely looking for me. Then, a fellow citizen suggested me to go to the Caritas. There I found a nice priest, who had taken care of me. A group of voluntaries gave me some clothes and got me in touch with my mother, who I have not heard nor seen for long time. Father Francesco gave me a job as a caregiver. I had to help an old woman who lived alone. The wage was low, but she offered me a roof and the possibility to call my mother sometimes. She was an invalid old woman, very sweet and sympathetic who soon loved me. However, unfortunately she died few months later. I remained homeless again and father Francesco could not find another job for me. A friend I had met on the street hosted me for short in an old, crumbling flat in CastelVolturno, where she was living with other Nigerians. I accepted, waiting for a better solution, but the things were not clear. I could see a strange traffic, strange and unknown people who came in and out of that house. I soon understood that I would have been again in trouble, unless I ran away as if my trouble were not enough. I did not know where to go. I could not imagine what was going to happen.

When the police came inside it was five o'clock in the morning, everyone was sleeping. We had woken up by a terrible mess, furious hits at the front door. I was terribly scared. They had searched every corner of the house. I did not know what they were looking for, nor what they had found, maybe drug. They had arrested all of us. I do not use these things, I only want to come back home. Can you help me to come back to my country? Arienzo, 1997

TERRY

The inspector of the Police went towards me, along the hallway of the first section. "Mrs" she said, "the prisoner who arrived yesterday is a little strange. Do you want to see her?". "Why? What's wrong with her?" She did not answer. However, she had an astonished face, as who doesn't know what to say. "It should be better to see her." She added." Bring her to my office".

Soon after the inspector came in with a strange type, tall and massive, with a bad shadowed beard, a pale hollowed face, long hair, uncared and collected on the neck. She had curved shoulders; prominent belly and she was wearing a worn-out pair of jeans and a dirty ripped shirt. "She is Terry C., the prisoner arrived yesterday," the inspector said. I looked upset at that strange human being of a unique appearance, but soon I realized it was not the case to be surprized over. The penalty institute environment is a place where the most unusual and emblematic cases of derelict and desperate humanity exist all together. Ambiguous and indefinite sexual people are not rare, people with so chaotic gender identity that even themselves have difficulty to understand.

From the first jail dialogue with Terry, nothing in particular emerged. She answered to some questions in a lazy way and with total indifference. She did not give any news on herself; she only asked to be employed in some job activities, to spend her time and to earn something. She explained she had a special attitude in electrotechnics and stonework. The day after, I studied her oversized biographic booklet, so I learnt that Terry C was born in Ostuni in 1952. She had arrived in prison 24 years before to expiate a penalty of six years, but she had never come out. During the period of detention, she had collected several crimes and a series of sentences, for an amount of 27 years to be expiate.

She had another name, at the moment of the first arrest. "My name was Federico", she told me, few days later. "I was very young and I worked as a trainer in an electrical workshop, but I earned very little money. I worked only to learn my job. I was a shy and timid boy, with few friends and a great fear to face with life. I envied my joyful and mellow peers, who had fun, laughing or dancing with girls. I was not like them; I felt frustration, dissatisfaction which have never left me and I was overwhelmed by a thin feeling of sadness. I felt myself inconsistent, unsuitable for everything and for everyone, without understand the reason.

Everything started when they arrested me by a misunderstanding, for rape, which I had never done. I do not know why that girl lied, accusing me and saving the real criminal. I had always declared my innocence, but judges had always believed to her words. I hardly knew her. She was nineteen and sometimes I used to meet her at night, while I was walking down the street of Ostuni, talking about nothing in particular, just to say something. That night I was alone. My friends had gone to the cinema and I had no money for the ticket. I had met her for chance. She was alone, too. We walked together, talking about nothing in particular. Then she went away, because she had a date, she did not say with whom. Some days later, she denounced me, declaring I convinced her, hardly forced her to follow me in a private place and then I would have raped her, but it was a lie. I liked that girl, even if she was not beautiful. She had sweet and vivid eyes and I was nearly falling in love with her. However, after that, I had hated

102

her, asshole, her, too, as everyone. At the trial, there were no witnesses, no proofs, but hey condemned me, even at the appeal.

Into the jail, at the beginning I was taken isolated, worrying for the attacks of other prisoners. You know, jail is not easy for prisoner accused of such crimes, like mine. They are considered shameful; they are not accepted and they believe to have the right to punish who had done such terrible guilt. I was alone in my cell without any contacts with anyone, except for the staff. I did not care about the solitude; on the contrary, I preferred it. Besides, I suffered for the accuse and penalty I had received. I had felt surrounded by hostility, persecuted by gazes, the whole world became intolerable to me. There was a big bitterness inside of me, which I could express only violently, a violence which I showed against the others and myself, too. I made many selfharms and several rushes. I let off steam in this way.

If I had had a good lawyer, maybe things would have gone differently, but my relative had not so much money and, to say the truth, they had left me alone. After all, my father had never loved me. He considered me as a bad son, not very clever and less talented. My brothers detested me and they never considered me at all. Only my mother loved me, feeling sad about my misfortune, even if she could do very little for me. She came to the jail talks, trying to support me. She brought me clean linen and something to eat. After her death, I remained alone.

The prison where I had been was awful, dark, crumbling, and unhealthy. The walls were humid; windows were placed on the top, making me see only the sky. The officers were like walls: hard, turned nasty, always ready to give reproaches. Staying there means losing once own personal freedom, but above all, feeling a psychological loneliness, the lack of love, the impossibility to communicate. The methodical flowing of time, according to the rules set up by others, fixed time for sleeping, for the waking up, for meals, for cleaning; gates everywhere, checking and pats down, continually.

After few weeks of detention, I was desperate and deeply depressed. Surely, I could not tolerate that condition for many years. I felt I would not have gone out anymore. Even if it had happened, without any aim, any future, what sense would it have, living to survive?

One morning I woke up early, but it was still dark. No sign of life could be perceived throughout the armoured gate that closed the cell. I looked up to the sky: it was dark as my soul. I took a bed sheet, I tore it, getting some strips, which I tided them up, making a sort of a chord. I twisted one end by my neck, and then I got up on a chair. I knotted the other end in the tallest horizontal bar of the gate at the window and I let myself fall down in the emptiness. When I woke up, I saw everything around me was white: walls, bed, blankets, furniture. I had a little plastic tube coming out from my nose and a paralyzed arm by a needle of intravenous feeding, put in a vein. A strong pain in my neck enabled me to turn my head. There were no other beds inside the room. I gave a glance to the bottom of the room and I saw two police officers, watching over me, perplexed. One of them went out, coming soon after with a young and kind doctor. I remember she smiled at me. It was the first smile I had received after a long time. She examined my eyes, measured my pressure blood, she looked inside my mouth and she checked my neck carefully. Then she asked my name, age, and other things. I answered with difficulty. My voice barely went out. She nodded at each answer, as I was a player in a quiz show. "You are lucky," she said." We have barely saved you". "I am not lucky", I answered. She looked me upset, but she did not say a word.

When I went out of the hospital, I came back to the prison, and after few days, they moved me to Brindisi. There I found a good social worker who was interested to my case. Even the captain was a good person. He soon employed me as a worker, responsible of the building maintenance. Working has always been therapeutic. Responsibility gave me a diversion. It helped me not to think and to control my emotion. I painted all the offices, several hallways, and the entrance hall. I was satisfied of that activity and of the captain's approval. I repaired doors and furniture, electrical systems, taps and fittings. I have always had good attitude for this kind of works. I was the only one able to do it, and it was satisfying for me.

However, there was an officer with a surly appearance, who could not stand me. He persecuted and reproached me continually. "You cannot do it, don't touch that! You must not go there! Don't stop there" I hated him, because he hated me and I did not understand why. To say the truth, he behaved in a bothersome way with all the prisoners: he had a jailer's soul. He seemed to be happy of others' misadventures. He was cruel, even if he was a low abiding.

One day I was repairing a syphon in a bathroom at the ground floor, when he came and took me into my cell. It was lunchtime. I had almost finished, it would have lasted few minutes to the end of the work. I had only to screw a bolt. "Leave everything and come to the canteen. It's time to lunch." He said. "Wait!" I answered. "Few minutes and I will finish."

"No. Leave it and come." He replied. "I have almost finished." "It doesn't matter, hurry up! Come on!" He shouted. "If you do not hurry up, I will make a report to the Captain about your behaviour." I got angry and I began to shout, me too. "Asshole, shit, son of a bitch!" I threw tweezers against him, hitting his temple. He lost little blood, but after all, I did not hurt him too much. I felt a little satisfaction, seeing his pale and frightened face. It was the end of the world. He denounced me to the Judiciary Authority for outrage and injury to a public officer. They kept me in isolation for three days and moved me to Foggia.

There, I was very bad. There was no work; the cells were little and uncomfortable: the walking area was a kind of courtyard with no sun nor light. I did not want to stay there and since I had understood the easy way to be moved, I put on practice my experience and I gave a slap on an officer's face, who, to say the truth, did not make me anything in particular.

Therefore, I arrived in Bari. That prison seemed another world: big, well organized, with many works and several pleasure activities. There was a comprehensive school, a professional course for electricians and another for lathe turner. Surely, my bad reputation had preceding me, since officers, instructors and all the staff looked at me with mistrust. The only kind person was the Chaplain, a young priest dynamic and full of initiatives, who spent his time for all of us. He made me follow a course of catechism, because he wanted me to confirm my catholic religion.

For the first time, they set me in a cell with other two prisoners. One of them was an idiot, the other, Gino, a great overbearing person. We had to tide his bed, to clean the bathroom, to buy coffee and cigarettes for him.

He was a crook. Inside that prison, there were many crooks, and his behaviour showed it clearly. He was assertive, tall, massive and full of tattoos. He had been many years in prison and he was so strong that he frightened all of us. Nobody tried to contrast him. I had complained about his behaviour with all officers, but they ignored me.

At the trial for outrage and injury to the public officer, they condemned me for three years of prison. I was discouraged. That penalty was added to the preceding ones and my hope to go out was getting far, more and more. Gino and I were following the course for electricians. One morning he woke me up very early, pretending me to clean the cell, to wash his working coverall and to prepare his coffee. That special waking upset and exasperated me, already very stressed. I went to the lab angry and bothered. During the lesson, while I was handling a screwdriver, I had an idea. I got closer Gino and, while he was working curved on his electrical system, I put the screwdriver into his shoulder. Shouts, disorder, and chaos: he lost his senses and the teacher was terrified. Some fellows immobilized me while others were laughing. Officials ran inside, but they could only certify what had happened.

I felt a sense of relief from a big weight. I thought they would move me again to another prison, as usual.

On the contrary, they moved me in a judiciary psychiatric hospital in Barcellona, Pozzo di Gotto, in Sicily. It was a mix of a jail and a mental institute. There were gates and metal grills, but even doctors, nurses, wheelchairs, special beds to tide those who got in crises, but it had never happened to me, because they gave me sedatives to make me quiet. I cannot say to have been well there, but there was more tolerance. I could behave in a strange or aggressive way and no one made reproach or denounce. They treated us as fools, and fools, you know, are odd. At least, they told us some words of sympathy or commiseration.

The atmosphere was not joyful, of course. There were strange people. I remember one who did not eat almost anything. They fed him by intravenous drip, but he ingested whatever he could: inedible pieces of glass, bolts, screws, pens, and nails. As a fakir, he used to ingest everything without worrying about consequences. Sometimes they recovered him in the hospital and they got all those harmful things from his stomach or they made him a surgery. He had had three or four surgeries, but he went on doing it: he had particular preference for metal objects, not excluding other materials, if only solid. Another one, besides, used to laugh: always. He used to roar with hysterical and upset laughers, night and day. When they gave him sedatives, he laughed less, but he never stopped, nor during his sleeping. I did not understand why he laughed so much and that got me angry. People told me he had slit a whore's throat, laughing.

I had been in Barcellona for three months, then Police brought me in Bari again. That time they set me in a single cell. I would have met the Chaplain again, followed his course of catechism, but I had no time, because few days later, I was sent to Vasto, then to Pescara, Chieti and Sulmona. At the trial for Gino's injuries, they gave me two years and six months of penalty. The Public Prosecutor wanted a sentence for attempted murder.

Then, I was sent to Aquila, where they got me angry, I did not remember why. I broke all the furniture inside the cell with the handle of a broom. Maybe it did not happen in Aquila, but in Campobasso, I did not remember well. In Ascoli Piceno, I had a stomach pump, because I had ingested some bleach, attempting to kill myself. In Potenza, I punched a doctor who did not want to give me a sedative. However, it is useful to list all the institute where I had been, the mistakes I had made and the consequent penalties I had received.

Yesterday, the psychologist told me I made all those crimes because I do not want to get out of prison. On his opinion, I am afraid to face with difficulties and daily problems of the external world. They scare me, so that even if life in prison is not nice at all, I am frightened to be worse outdoor. He said I feel protected inside. Maybe he is right, I do not know. After all, we all have a reason to do what we do.

Maybe it is true that I do not want to get out. I have never been at easy among people whenever I went, whomever I met. What had never abandoned me was a sense of inner discomfort, a continue sadness, which I felt everywhere and with everyone. I have always felt in the wrong place, excluded, alone, far from the other interests. World was unknown for me. What had surrounded me seemed a context in which I was put there for mistake. I was a Martian who, got down on the earth, cannot understand the sense of human life. Competitions with other prisoners to get the power inside the cell or inside a section, the strategies to keep supervisors' benevolence or favours, had always been stupid things for me. Even among the officers and all the staff, there are hidden or clear contexts to get prestige, which, at the end, get nowhere. Inside myself, there was a desire to isolate, to stay far from other miseries.

In Salerno, my life changed radically. There I met Alberto. He was an accountant, arrested for tax fraud or a swindle, I do not remember. I was together with him inside the same cell. He was a gentleman, well educated. He could speak well and he knew laws. All the prisoners and officers respected him, taking him in great consideration. He took me under his protection, explaining me many situations, which were incomprehensible before. He taught me how to behave in some circumstances, with some people. At the end, I felt no more alone. I had a support, a point of reference, someone to ask for help, love and solidarity. It is difficult to explain these things. Moreover, it is difficult to understand them. I fell in love with Alberto. I felt lost without him. I used to look for him. I was enchanted by his voice and words, while he spoke with others. I was happy because he made me feel calm. I was waiting for his nodding glance or loving gesture towards me, as a child uses to do with his mother. I think he had never noticed it. Maybe it will seem ridiculous all that, but you have to understand that when you stay for a long time here inside, judgments change totally and what is important for the external world, it does not exist anymore. The only important thing is what happens inside the microcosm of the jail.

Unfortunately, Alberto went away soon, and I fell down into a deep depression, from which I got out only after a long time. However, for me there had been a revelation: I had realized what that sense of distress, that deep and unexplained sense of sadness was, which oppressed me. My sex was wrong. I had soul, feelings, and spirit of a woman.

Nature had played a bad role: I should have been born a woman, so I should become a woman. I started to remove my hairs, to put make up, to behave and dress as a woman, to have my hair long, that I made golden blond. Others looked at me astonished, someone laughed at me, others felt sorry, others tried to rope me, but I did not accept sexual relationships with anyone. I became a problem for the security officers. They tried to keep me alone, looking at me with suspicious or uncertainty. I had talked about that with the psychologist, with instructors, but nobody gave importance to my case. They considered it as an odd behaviour of an odd prisoner. Homosexual or transsexual problems inside jail are put apart carefully or considered problems to be ignored or censuring depravations. I did not stop. I would like to become a woman. I came back to the topic with everyone, with officers, social assistant, vice director. I broke a wardrobe for medicine inside the infirmary. I tried twice suicide and I hit everyone who had laughed at me.

During my several transfers, from an institute to another for disciplinary sanctions, I obsessed all the doctors and specialists by my requests, my questions, my doubts until one of them, exasperated, wrote something on the medical folder, concluding with the sentence: "he would like to change his sex." Changing sex: that had been my one- track mind, my greatest desire for ten years. I was convinced that if I could have got my target, everything would have changed. I would have been better with myself and my eternal sense of distress and unhappiness would have been vanished. I used to speak with everyone, with my fellows, officers, with staff, and everyone used to listen to me with sceptical indifference.

When I arrived in the prison of Turin, a doctor took in consideration my desire. He realized my deep desperation had made my life intolerable. He studied my personality for long; I had several interviews with him, during which I explained my feelings, my anxiety and my agony. At the end, he filled a detailed report he sent to the Ministry. Several specialists from the hospital, such as sexologists, psychologists, surgeons came and made me fill in questioners, tests and so on. They visited me carefully. It was an endless period of preparation for me.

At the end, they recovered me in the hospital in Turin, where I started a long series of exams, check, interviews and other preliminaries. I was afraid that all at once, the surgery would be impossible. Besides, it was not so. It was a complex surgery, which took many hours and a long recovering. After a month, I was dismissed and I came back to prison. I was set in a single cell inside the female section. I was satisfied and plenty of wishing; now my life would have changed deeply and I could have got the inner balance I had always missed. I could behave in a normal way, according my personality without making the other laughing. I needed a sentence of Courthouse to sign up my sex changing and my new name on anagraphic document.

The first meeting with women inside the jail was very difficult. Since then, I had always had few contacts with female genre, few relationships, mostly disastrous. I found myself among whores, viragos, liars, fakers, but even among unlucky poor evils, victims and dominating people. A mix of women very different from men, with whom I had been in touch. They were intrusive, curious and aggressive, but more determined and intuitive. I noticed in particular the absolute lack of inhibition of some. I had never seen so much vulgarity. Many of them despised, insulting and telling every kind of outrageous adjectives to me. However, I used to pretend not to hear them, even if those insults made me feel humiliated and suffering.

Besides, others showed humanity, comprehension, being generous of advices.

I felt tied with one of them in particular. She was a whore, who had robbed a customer. She was well educated; she used to read a lot. She taught me how to put make up and choose the right cloths. She would have liked to give me cooking lessons, but I had always been denied. I cannot cook an egg. She gave me a book written by a transsexual, titled "A different woman" or something similar, but it was helpless. I did not understand very much, and I did not care what I understood.

I had had many expectations from that surgery. Maybe too many. Firstly, I would have liked to find my real personality, and then, I would have been ease at other people and self-confident, being integrated within a world I had always felt unknown, getting out of my depression, which never left me.

I went on with my psychotherapy and with hormonal cures. I studied my fellows' behaviour and I tried to explore their mind. I read love novels and female magazines. I spoke about famous singers, handsome actors, sensual actress, who did not attract me at all, about songs and TV programs which I pretend to appreciate. Following their example, I read horoscopes, I learnt recipes and I was on a diet, which was useless. I liked love novels but I did not identify myself in the main character, who hardly always was beautiful, young and blonde. Obviously, I was so far from those pictures. I did not hope to become beautiful. I wanted only to recognize myself as a woman.

I was waiting for my female identity coming out, and my personality finally balanced with my body, to become a complete woman. My soul was ready to accept the change as the result of the transformation done. I had been waiting for this expectation for long and I had spent so long in this waiting.

Then, one day, I realized what I had thought for long: nothing had happened. The surgeon, the psychotherapy, the cures, the doctors, the sympathy, my constancy, everything had been useless. My deep and unexplained dissatisfaction, that indefinite sensation of useless, that feeling of being an outsider, always and everywhere, had still remained untouched.

I realized it was not my sex, not that, the reason of my eternal laziness, impatience, towards the others, that sense of lack of interests towards any side of life, that sense of annoyance, which had always followed me everywhere and in every circumstance. It had been an illusion the need to find a reason for that emptiness, which this strange way of being created inside and around me. It had misled me. I decided to put on male clothes again, to stop my hormonal cures, the interviews with psychologists and checking controls. I was no more worried about my physical appearance. It had no sense. Nothing had importance, anymore. I should fit myself with my unhappiness, because I could have never destroyed it. What remains of this experience is only the name: Terry! There was something painful in my soul, which no one had been able to get it off. It was clear at that point that this problem would have always been hidden deep in the darkest bottom of my soul.

Arienzo 1999.

ELISA

Tall, slender, hazel eyes and a cloud of curly copper-coloured hair that framed her face, Elisa never smiled. Her dark and thoughtful expression denounced a constant anguish that disappeared only when she spoke of little Imma, her daughter. Her way of speaking revealed a discreet culture and a rather distinct behavior, the result of evident bourgeois origins. She was born and grown up in a residential district of Naples, in a wealthy family who had educated her according to traditional criteria.

Unfortunately, fate had taken her away from the understandable plans of her parents by taking her on a completely different path. Her existence had been upset by a disastrous marriage that she had contracted when she was still too young to suspect the deceptions that can be hidden behind an apparent happiness. «When I met Saverio, I was seventeen. He came from a village in the province, attended my own school and was a few years ahead. I had noticed that he was looking at me insistently, but I did not care much. One day I was in the courtyard of the institute, together with the crowd of the other students, waiting for the bell to enter the classroom. I was discussing with a friend about the classroom assignment of the day before, when I felt myself vigorously pulling my hair from behind. I turned suddenly and I saw him, he had an ironic and easy-going expression.

"Are they true? ' she said. "What?'- I asked. "The hair, are they real? They look like a wig with all those curls and that strange color: '" But how does such a thing come to your mind?' I answered resentfully, but then I laughed. He laughed too and after a few minutes, it was as if we had

115

known each other forever. I was young, naive and dreamer, like all the girls of that age and I thought I had found my Prince Charming. A modern prince, with blond hair a little long, a sparkle in his ear, a nice appearance and an expensive and powerful motorbike with which we toured all over Naples. I hugged him, on that means with jeans and a waterproof jacket and, regardless of the heat and bad weather I followed him everywhere, in Posillipo, via Caracciolo, Mergellina and in many other romantic places in the city. Then, in the summer, we began to go further up to the coast. We slipped on the road defying the wind that slapped the face and the sun beating on the head, happy to bathe in the waters of Positano or to eat in some small restaurant in Sorrento. Not that I ignored those places, but with him everything took on another aspect, another dimension, whatever he said seemed interesting and amusing to me, it made me laugh and made me feel serene. It was probably just suggestion because now thinking about him in hindsight, I only see a squalid and mean person.

It was inevitable that my parents would know about this story, on the other hand I did nothing to hide it, I found nothing strange, many of my friends had a boyfriend with the tacit consent of families. They too, at first, silently tolerated my exits, but then my father began to investigate and get information, and that was how the war broke out in the house. My father revealed to me that Saverio came from a family with a bad reputation who was viewed with great diffidence in his country. I did not believe it for a while, it all seemed nonsense to me, who knows who had provided the absurd news, certainly some malevolent person. My boyfriend was polite, kind, sensitive, none of what they wanted me to believe could be true, and then what did he have to do with the family? My father's arguments seemed to me pretentious and exaggerated, dictated by prejudice and by the desire to exercise exclusivity over me and not by an objective ability to analyze things. On the other hand, he was not new to these behaviors; he always had to complain about anything I did. These were the thoughts that whipped in my mind and blurred my reason. I even proposed to my parents to meet Saverio, to find out who he was but they obviously refused insisting on trying in vain to convince me that the relationship would only cause me troubles.

With this premise, my life became unsustainable, I was prevented from going out to meet him and at home, the atmosphere was an oppressive and unbearable hood. Every reason was good to unleash my father's anger as my mother closed herself more and more in a mutism, full of unspoken reproaches. My brother Guido, who until a short time before had been a valid partner of mine in all family conflicts, avoided me like a plague by not daring to express opinions.

I think this way of acting was a big mistake of mine; all they did was move further and further away from them, creating at home a hostile and intolerable environment from which I only wanted to escape. I was pushed more and more towards Saverio, who had become my only peaceful landing, even if we could see very little. I was just eighteen years old when he, to get away from that situation of conflict in the family, asked me to get married without the consent of my parents, placing me, in fact, in front of an ultimatum.

I could not imagine my life without him and I accepted. None of my relatives was present at the wedding. My father closed definitively with me, even just saying my name was forbidden. Guido followed his father's direction and disappeared from my life. Later, by accident, I learned that he had married, but until a few days ago, I didn't even know what his wife' name. My mother was overwhelmed with pain that she became seriously ill and died some time later. This event further alienated my brother who, having caused me a few feelings of guilt, has always considered me the main responsible for that misfortune. I went to live in my husband's country with his family, an authentic tribe, called Marras tribe. The house was, and still is, a large shapeless and rather austere building, without any aesthetic claim on the outside but comfortable enough on the inside. The construction, in tuff stone, completely devoid of decorative elements or unnecessary tinsel, is made up of over three floors and is defined by all as "The Villa". It is surrounded by a large park, also very austere, a kind of grove, mainly consisting of poplars and eucalyptus, without flowers or ornamental plants. The villa was a kind of meeting place where all the members of the family met and sometimes clashed, with a continuous and constant frequency that involved people of all ages. The concept of family for the Marras was very extensive and did not only include uncles, cousins, grandchildren, but also a rather complex set of relationships and ties that went far beyond simple kinship.

Saverio's family in the strict sense was made up of a mother, father, brother and two sisters. My mother-in-law, Immacolata, welcomed me with reserve, without particular affection or aversion. Even if she wanted the marriage immediately, to protect the respectability of the name, she maintained an attitude of observation towards me as if she expected from me a proof of unquestionable loyalty. She was an authoritarian woman who did not allow replies to her decisions. She demanded control and the last word on everything that happened around her. In every corner of the house, her presence was felt. Her eyes searched all inquiringly as if to steal the innermost thoughts. She was very religious, never neglected Sunday mass, recited the rosary at least once a day and had posted a crucifix in every room. The rituals she made were of pure exteriority; however, she carried them out assiduously, convinced that they would give him a privileged treatment by the Eternal Father. She had an Old Testament conception of God, a vindictive and quick-tempered God ready to inflict punishment and disaster on every human being guilty of even the slightest sin. I could not stand that woman so cumbersome, but I feared her a lot and I had the unpleasant sensation of being constantly under her surveillance.

My father-in-law, Don Raffaele, as everyone called him, instead was apparently very helpful and friendly. He acted as someone who stands above all, behaving as an enlightened patriarch who everything understands and solves. In truth, he was highly esteemed by friends and relatives who frequented the Villa; all showed respect and held his opinions and judgments in high regard. However, I could perceive a strange ambiguity and I felt an incomprehensible mistrust towards him. Maybe, my father's word created my unjustified doubts unconsciously. He always used to surround himself by trusted men who accompanied him everywhere, never left him alone. Among them, a certain Gino, a stocky, muscular individual, full of tattoos with a grim look that spoke very little.

Saverio's first sister, Bianca, was worthy of being a full member of the Adams family. Dark skin, raven hair, pitch eyes, a long skeletal figure dressed in mournful clothes made her appearance almost ghostly, in stark contrast to that name, Bianca, imposed by the observance of family traditions. The internal aspect was not different from the external one; it had a dark and unfriendly character and continuously elaborated malicious thoughts. Her susceptibility led her to suspect that the whole world was plotting against her for unspecified purposes. Fortunately, she cared little about me as she was constantly engaged in two jobs: embroidery and crochet. She skilfully executed splendid works, authentic works of art, which recalled the skill of embroiderers of the past and which engaged her for whole days. She prepared the outfit for his younger sister: not only sheets, blankets, tablecloths, but also paintings, rugs, curtains, all made with tireless hyena.

His brother, Rocco, was a huge and big man, rough in appearance and behavior. He was married to Elena: a rather vulgar woman whose main characteristic was an excessive inclination for gossip, so, as to often arouse the resentment of Immacolata, a person full of defects but discreet as a grave. Elena had no sympathy for me, it was clear, on the other hand, the sentiment was cordially reciprocated. The two lived in a neighboring town and, unlike others, they came very little to the Villa. However, he was always with his father when it came to deciding important matters.

The only person who had attracted my sympathy and my trust was Saberio's last sister, Dora, a cordial and lively 20-year-old girl, blonde-haired woman, with large hazel eyes littered with golden specks, minute features and a gorgeous physique, in short, an authentic beauty. She studied architecture at university and had far expectations from her family projects. The country was tight as a straitjacket and she had understandable hopes of escape. She imagined her life in some northern city if not even abroad and her work in some multinational company or in an important advertising graphics studio. She was happy and full of fantasy, she loved cinema, trips to the sea, music, and she never missed the big concerts in Piazza del Plebiscito in Naples. She had a particular fondness for whimsical clothes and stiletto heels. In her apparent lightness, Dora was intelligent and sensitive; she could feel the sufferings of others and identified herself with their problems. Her desire to live was tolerated in the family like the liveliness of a capricious little girl. Bianca looked at that sister, so different from her, with glances of mild reproach but with indisputable love, while her mother, overwhelmed by her exuberance, indulged her pretending to contrast her.

She was promised to Giacomo, a young surveyor son of his father's friend, a rough and insignificant type with rather limited perspectives who expressed himself almost always in an incomprehensible dialect. Their engagement had never been officially formalized and their relationship was practically nonexistent. I often saw him wandering around the house looking for attention while she ignored him.

After a first period of adaptation I got used to the life that took place in the villa, to the coming and going of people who circulated in various ways and to their children who scattered in every corner with a rather noisy invasion that no one cared about to contain. All those people did not interest me, just as I was not interested in the activity of my father-in-law who traded in bricks and building materials, nor did I believe that everything that happened around concerned me. I did not dwell much on even half-sibling phrases and speeches that I happened to hear, even if they gave me strange unpleasant sensations. The only luxury Marras

121

allowed was the service staff. They had cooks, gardeners and domestic workers of all kinds who provided for the many needs. Therefore, I saw myself exonerated from annoying housework and I found myself completely idle. I thought about resuming the studies that I had abandoned after the wedding, but I never decided seriously to consider the possibility. Saverio had left the university to take care of his father's business. He began to learn the management techniques of the company and dedicated all his free time to me. We often went to Naples with friends to see some theatrical performances. There was no shortage of invitations to dinners or ceremonies welcomed without enthusiasm, mostly as obligations to be fulfilled.

I had not yet adapted to living in that country and in that house when something very strange happened which I did not then examine with the necessary attention.

A strong explosion in the middle of the night ripped through the silence. I woke up suddenly and frightened jumped out of bed, the phosphorescent hands of the alarm clock marked three. I realized that Saverio was not sleeping, the light on his bedside table was on and he had an open book in front of him. "What happened?"- I asked frightened. "Nothing," he replied with ill-concealed calm. What do you mean nothing? Something must have happened. "" Of course, but it doesn't seem appropriate to rush to the street at this time of night to go and see. Sleep now, tomorrow morning we will know: 'The speech, from the logical point of view, did not make a wrinkle but I was surprised by its almost angry tone.

I went back under the covers but I could no longer sleep a wink. A few minutes later, in the distance, I could hear the hiss of the sirens of the police cars and the police. The next day I learned that the blast had occurred in an appliance store. "A gas leak," said Saverio, who, for the rest, was very stingy with information by replying several times with a generic "I don't know". There was no mention of the fact in the family. Indeed everyone carefully avoided commentary. Under the cushion of a sofa, I found a newspaper reporting the news, so I learned that it had not been a gas leak at all but an explosive charge placed inside the shop, perhaps for intimidating purposes. The owner probably refused to pay for the lace. Luckily, there had been no victims but the place and all the goods had been destroyed and the owner, a certain Vincenzo Todisco, was reduced to the brink. The dynamics of that fact, Saverio's lie, the hidden newspaper and the Marra's attitude of mystery aroused a certain amazement in me but I did not suspect and I avoided investigating. Dora confessed to me that she fell in love with a fellow student, Luca, a contemporary biology student, who had conquered her heart. She told me their story, how they had met and how they understood they were made for each other. Since they had been together for almost a year, they had decided to formalize the relationship. "So far I have kept everyone in the dark but now," he said, "I have to reveal it, I can no longer keep this secret, I am telling you that because I know you can understand me and advise me. He too has decided to speak with his people." "How are you going to do with Giacomo?" I asked. She looked at me almost surprised at my observation, then went silent thoughtfully for a few minutes: "I absolutely have to talk to my mother", she said after a while "Do you think she will understand?" I asked worried. "She'll have to understand, everyone will have to understand, I never considered Giacomo my boyfriend, I can't stand him, in fact I hate him, he is an insidious and mean person and then we never got engaged officially. I cannot accept and I do not want to suffer a husband imposed by conferences and agreements between families'. Dora was unable to persuade her family and, after a stormy conversation with her mother, she was prevented from going out and communicating with her boyfriend. The atmosphere in the villa became dark and heavy. It reminded me of what had been created in my house in similar circumstances well known to me. She locked herself in her room sinking into despair. I was the only person with whom she agreed to speak but I could not give her useful advice nor could I help her because I too was under close surveillance, everyone feared that I could act as an intermediary between the two lovers. Which I actually tried to do but with many difficulties. Giacomo was gone, he never showed up again, and this seemed to me the only positive aspect of the situation, on the other hand, his father, who kept himself for hours in interminable secret speeches with Don Raffaele, appeared much more often.

In this context, one day I realized I was expecting a child. The news fell in an unhappy moment and nobody was particularly impressed. Only my mother-in-law, in a rush of emotion, commented: "We can't even celebrate with the problem we have- 'I wanted to ask her what problem could create the fact that her daughter instead of a rude, stupid, wanted to marry a decent, educated young man, who loved her, but I didn't dare to speak. I would have understood later what extent that problem was.

Pregnancy, especially in the early days, brought me a lot of trouble, nausea, and vomiting, back pain. I spent most of my days in bed or in an armchair in my room, avoiding the villa goers. Dora's situation, despite the passing of months, was unchanged; she had shown a stubbornness that her parents did not imagine. Of course, they had underestimated the character of that daughter who had always been treated as a capricious child. The screams and quarrels were frequent, my mother-in-law was more and more intractable, Don Raffaele, behind an impenetrable expression concealed an obvious nervousness and Dora had become pale and gaunt like a rag. One afternoon, Saverio entered the room with his face red and his eyes out of his sockets. "She ran away she said." How ... ran away? 'I repeated dumbfounded. "Yes, yes, she ran away, in her room she is not there and she took many things away. Now I try to catch her again" "But what do you say, catch her again? - I replied, "Where do you think you're going to run? At his house? She is not necessarily there. Your sister is of age, you cannot all treat her like a brat. She didn't even answer me and ran away like a fury."

A few days earlier Dora had mentioned something to me. "I'm doing the same as you," she said, "I'm leaving." However, it did not seem serious to me and anyway I was careful not to tell anyone. A few hours later, Saverio managed to bring her home in the grip of an indescribable hysterical crisis. However, the worst was yet to come and came when that unconscious feeling that there was something shady in my father-in-law's business turned into certainty. It happened on a Sunday afternoon. They had all gone out, Saverio to the stadium and the others I do not know; I had stayed in the upstairs room, suffering from the usual ailments due to pregnancy. The villa appeared unusually uninhabited, the service staff enjoyed rest and only Dora, perennially locked in her room, and Don

Raffaele, who reunited with some friends in the living room on the ground floor, were in the house. Complaining about the absence of the cook, I decided to go down to the kitchen to prepare a chamomile tea. I had now become rather heavy and this forced me to move carefully so as not to run the risk of falling. At the foot of the stairs I heard my father-in-law and his friends in the next room discuss animatedly ... The voices were clearly perceived, even if the content of their speeches seemed rather hazy.

Rocco occasionally raised his tone to reduce it immediately after almost to a whisper. Intrigued, I stopped to listen more carefully, the sentences arrived fragmented and incomplete, the language was ambiguous but the references were understandable and their meaning gradually began to take shape without the possibility of misunderstanding. Trafficking, bribes, exploitation, extortion and more: that is the subject of those speeches. Circumstances, facts, places, names, were examined in detail for the development and implementation of specific criminal designs. I heard several surnames pronounced several times, including that of Vincenzo Todisco, the appliance dealer. Paralyzed by fear and annihilated by the discovery, I remained motionless in that corner at the foot of the staircase behind the living room wall, for, I do not know how long, without having the courage to move a muscle and forced to listen to everything. Before they found me, I found the strength to go up as quietly as possible and went back exhausted to my room.

It is difficult to describe the agony of the following days and the torment of long sleepless nights spent thinking about my future and that of the creature I was about to give birth. An unimaginable scenario had opened up on my life. I had to recognize that, unfortunately, my father was not wrong, but what worried me most was the relationship with my husband. Suddenly I saw him in a disquieting perspective; I wondered how far he participated in his father's activities and how he could disguise himself with such skill. I worked out a great resentment towards him. it was an unconscious fool who had dragged me, an unwary eighteen year old girl, into that environment. And Dora? I had always considered her a loyal and worthy girl, she could not have known, perhaps for that reason she dreamed of changing the environment and leaving. Now I understood the meaning of some speeches and some allusions that I had heard and which, ignoring the premise, I could not understand. The appliance store episode also became easy to understand.

Pretending various ailments, I tried to avoid contact with all the members of the family, including Saverio, as if this could serve to keep me "outside" The misunderstandings began between us. I realized that some of his behaviours, which I was unaware to explain by superficiality or distraction, they had rather specific reasons. I could not stand him anymore and above all, I could not stand the family. Now Immacolata's privacy, Rocco's hostility, Bianca's distrust, Don Raffaele's ambiguity had clear explanations.

In those days, I knew by Guido that my mother was hospitalized in serious conditions at the hospital and she asked to see me. I knew that my father would not let me warn him but then he had bowed to the desire of his wife. With my body in pieces and soul in turmoil I ran to her, she was alone in the room, my father and brother had avoided meeting me. I approached the bed with a great feeling of pain in my heart and without uttering a word, I clasped her hands in mine. A glance was enough for her to understand that the fragile illusions on which I had built my life had disintegrated, but she did not reproach, she smiled sadly and a shadow of regret was painted on her face. We looked at each other for a long time and spoke to each other in the silent language of the glances. She could hardly breathe and her face had the white veins of marble. Then I realized that this was the last time I saw her.

This was only the first of a series of misfortunes that hit me at the time, leaving me prostrated on a physical and psychic level.

A few days had passed since my mother's end when one morning, together with Dora's excruciating screams, a gloomy atmosphere of oppression spread throughout the villa. My mother-in-law and my sister-in-law Bianca, pale and silent, were holed up in the kitchen, while Don Raffaele, Rocco, Saverio and others, locked up in the study, discussed excitedly. Gino stood guard at the door, checking that no one entered or listened. I ran to Dora and found her alone, lying on the bed, with her earthy face, her eyes wide and with her hands in her hair. "Luca is dead," he said as soon as he saw me. I did not believe my ears. "How did he die?' I sat terrified. She sat on the bed and with an improbable calm put her hands on her knees. For a few interminable minutes, her gaze was lost in the void and her face remained fixed in a stone expression. I approached her worried. "It was them," he said suddenly. "Them who?"- I asked unnecessarily, because I knew the answer well. "Giacomo? His father?"-I asked. "Everyone," she replied. I sat down next to her. "But how did it happen?" "Someone shot him on his way out of college to simulate a robbery." When? "" This morning, an hour ago ... maybe two ... I don't know "" How did you know?"- "A friend of mine called me a little while

128

ago. Her sudden change impressed me, that hallucinated calm was much worse than a hysterical crisis. Her face had lost all charm and her eyes had gone dull and lightless. She turned her gaze to me without seeing me. "How am I going to live with this scruple?" She said. A cover of frost completely enveloped me. I wanted to comfort her but I could not find the words, all this was too big for her and me. Giacomo had started to move around the house again, he had assumed a vaguely bossy air, seeing him, gave me a sense of repugnance. When he was there, Dora did not leave her room.

A wall had risen between Saverio and I. Nothing more linked each other. Displeased by my impatient attitude, he became aggressive and despotic. He spent more and more time away from home even after work and addressed me in arrogant ways. He no longer even worried about hiding the shady activities of his father, in which he too was entangled. I believe that I could never betray him, he discussed with the partners about his affairs even in my presence. He claimed to make me accept the situation as if it were an unavoidable necessity. Those dramatic events made the last period of pregnancy unbearable, but the conclusion was truly tragic. There were a couple of weeks left to give birth, finally a happy circumstance amidst many misfortunes, and I was not yet fully organized. The events of recent times had not allowed me to concentrate sufficiently on the event and so I had not finished preparing the layette for the little girl. I knew it would be a girl and Bianca had embroidered me with pink dresses, bibs and small sheets for the cot.

I was going to make the last purchases that morning: a donkey, a bottle, a bathrobe for the bath, and something else. I had dressed and was about to go downstairs. Immaculate, who had offered to accompany me, was waiting for me at the foot of the stairs. She decided to go to Dora first for a moment, went up to her daughter with a determined step. I followed her, moving slowly due to the weight and the tiredness, I saw her open the door, pause for a moment on the threshold of the room and then rush inside. Before I could reach her, she let out a chilling scream. Dora was lying on the floor with her glazed eyes, her body folded in on itself and her face contracted by the spasms of agony. On the bedside table, two empty boxes of a powerful sleeping pill revealed what had happened during the night. Immaculate was in desperation and in a state of shock, she did not connect and fidgeted like an automaton without making sense of her gestures. Paralyzed by terror and anguish, I remained a few moments as petrified; I felt my heart and stomach tighten in a painful grip. I approached Dora trying to understand her condition, panting I knelt on the floor, I felt the stabbing pains in the back and abdomen, the forces were abandoning me.

Exhausted I took her head in my arms. She had a waxy complexion and sweat-soaked hair, her light nightgown completely wet, adhering to the skin as cold as marble. I stroked her frozen forehead. "What did you do?' I said in a low voice. She stared at me with her gaze lost in nothing and opened her mouth slightly as if to say something to me, but immediately after she closed her eyes, her features relaxed and the pallor of death appeared on her face. Her body slipped from my hands, in a few moments it had turned to lead and I could no longer bear the weight. That moment has remained engraved in my memory and there is no day in my life when the diaphanous face of that girl does not appear before my eyes as she exhales her last breath. It is now a nightmare, a terrifying nightmare, that haunts me day and night and that I will never be able to erase from my mind.

Called by the screams, everyone rushed. Bewilderment, horror, pain, impotence spread throughout the house. In that situation of collective hysteria, someone called the ambulance, which arrived immediately.

It did not serve for Dora, but it was useful for me.

I arrived in hospital in very serious conditions, I was taken to the surgery room urgently and I was practiced caesarean section. The child was born asphyxiated and heavy bleeding seized me. Luckily, a good surgeon managed to stop. When days later I left the hospital with the girl in my arms, I felt miraculous.

The atmosphere in the house was severe and the tension palpable. My mother-in-law had worn mourning black clothes, had closed in an exasperating mutism and spent almost all the time immersed in prayer. Pale as a ghost, she spent hours in front of the photos depicting her smiling daughter. When she saw the little girl, she kissed her and stroked her with tenderness but then returned to her mystical isolation. Bianca resentful against the whole world was perennially concentrated on her embroideries that no longer served anyone and Don Raffaele spent almost the whole day closed in the study alone or with a few others. The service staff were also bewildered and nervous.

The villa was practically deserted, almost all the people who circulated in the past on the ground floor rooms, after the first visits of condolence, had disappeared, probably out of a sense of respect for the pain that oppressed the family. Only some of my father-in-law's lackeys, including

Gino, continued to act as his mob. Luckily, I had the little girl to think about, she absorbed all my time and attention. Immacolata proposed to call her Dora but Saverio was contrary. "It is not a lucky name," Grandmother's name was chosen in respect of tradition. My mother in law became morbidly attached to her granddaughter, who somehow had replaced her favourite daughter. The relationship between my husband and me was worsening over time. Quarrels and reproaches were on the agenda. I often stopped to examine the situation in which I found myself. I detested my husband and ALL of his clan and had definitively broken all ties with mine. I did not have a job; I did not have any income or family support to rely. Moreover, I had to take care of Imma. How to ask for separation? Saverio would not have worried about my maintenance; on the contrary, considering my financial condition and the staff of lawyers he had, he would have asked for and perhaps obtained the custody of his daughter. Then, in that environment it was not easy to act, I was not allowed to pack and go away with the little girl, as any other woman would have done.

As much as I tortured my mind, I could not find a way out of that cage. Irina was the name of my release. She was a tall, blonde, young Ukrainian with a top-model physique who came to the country as a caregiver for an elderly wealthy lady. Saverio literally lost his head for her and left traces of his betrayal everywhere. Placed in front of the evidence, he did not regret much and between me and her he chose her, indifferent to his protests. In Marras clan, the news created a mess. My mother-in-law knew very well that this circumstance would offer me the opportunity I had been waiting for some time. A foreigner, a kind of Martian, had come from another planet to bribe her son and drive her granddaughter away. For me, in fact, it was a providential and unexpected event, which allowed me to leave with the child, and to leave that house and that family forever. Saverio did not dwell much on the details of the separation, the only interest for him in that moment was Irina. Driven by his mother, he made it the only condition for me to stay in the country to give him the opportunity to see Imma often. I accepted; I could not afford to draw the wrath of the Marra on me; overall, I had already achieved a lot. He would pay me a monthly sum, rather small for the maintenance of his daughter and he did not intend to give me more, in fact, he was almost propertyless. Marra's patrimony, which had to be large, had to be cleverly concealed with standard gap strategies, in Swiss accounts, fictitious companies, figureheads and more.

It was very difficult to find accommodation. Few showed availability to give me accommodation. Then I found a lawyer Mr Russo. I had never heard of him in the environment I had lived until then and this seemed like a guarantee. He and his wife were humble and attentive people. They rented me a modest but dignified apartment in an old building located on the outskirts of the village. I think they were more convinced of pity than convenience, but I think they did not regret it because I always worried about paying regularly.

In that building, I finally found some peace and many friendly people, two in particular, Angela and Margherita.

Angela was an accountant looking for a stable job she will never find and mother of two teenage children. Her husband, often absent, worked in a big building company, always forced to follow the transfers of the building site to locations even quite distant. Margherita, after a first period of distrust, became my best friend. She was Stefano's wife, a good man without malice who owns a bar located in a rather central street. The restaurant had certainly experienced ancient splendours but over time, it had found itself in an inevitable state of decline. It would have required an effective restructuring and a minimum of maintenance that Stefano could not afford as tightly as he was in the grip of expenses, taxes and crime collectors who demanded increasingly exorbitant bribes, based on the assumption of huge gains that actually did not exist.

In the early days, he had also tried to help me by hiring me in the bar as a cashier but then he was no longer able to support the expense of albeit minimal salary. Fortunately, I found work in a kindergarten run by nuns, the wages were small but with that and with the money that Saverio paid me monthly I was able to go on. I even bought a car, a small second-hand subcompact that came in handy in certain circumstances.

Stefano was constantly threatened, they demanded commitments from him that he could not keep, twice at night he had damaged the room by breaking the shutter and introducing himself inside. Lately I often saw him distracted, thoughtless, surely something troubled him. Margherita would have liked to close everything and go away, but he did not feel like it, he had inherited that activity from his father and all his life he had done only that, he had managed a bar in his country and only that he could do. "And then 'he said," where would we go? What job could I do at my age? "

For some time Margherita was very worried. She lived in constant tension; everything frightened her. Poor woman, she was not wrong. Now she is alone and desperate. I am afraid for her, she is diabetic and sometimes the blood sugar levels skyrocket. What happened recently has severely damaged her health. About twenty days ago, another tile fell on my head and not just mine.

I was coming back from work and in the courtyard of the building I met Stefano who was running out, I said goodbye but he did not see me and he did not answer me, he was visibly upset. Bewildered I went up to the first floor by Angela who had taken on the task of hosting Imma upon returning from school until I returned. "I saw Stefano going out, he was upset 'I said to Angela as soon as she opened the door, but she didn't give me time to continue." The girl did not return from school, I immediately ran to the school and they told me that my grandmother went to pick her up. Now she must be at the villa, 'said in an alarmed tone. In recent years, Imma has become a beautiful wise and intelligent girl. It looks so much like Aunt Dora, same blonde hair and same golden specks in the hazel eyes. My mother-in-law has never resigned herself to the idea of staying away from her only granddaughter; she has always tried in every way to steal her, with threats and blandishments. She even offered me a huge sum of money as long as I left with her. Indeed, I have quite different ambitions, I do not care about Marra's money and I think I have shown it. What I want for my daughter is a peaceful life, a beautiful family, a prestigious but honest job and if there is money, it will be better, but it must be clean money.

Angela's words provoked me an annoyance. It was not the first time that Immacolata went to pick up the little girl at school without warning me, creating quite a few problems, since the villa is located at the opposite end of the town. Getting there means driving a long and busy stretch of road by car.

I rushed home, took the car keys and went down to the open space at the back of the building where I usually park the car. It is a small area with little access and bordering on private land planted with vegetables, which can also be accessible from the inside through the corridor of the basements. Contrary to the usual, the road was not very crowded and I arrived at my destination in a short time. The avenue leading to the main entrance of the villa was blocked by two large trees fallen during the storm of the day before, so I was forced to take a side road in clay that leads to the secondary entrance, through the park. At the edge of the park, I left my car to walk the path between the poplars and eucalyptus trees, and right there a few meters away I saw, among the trees, Stefano surrounded by three henchmen of Don Raffaele, including my brother in law Rocco and Gino. The three of them argued with him in an altered way, but I could not understand the terms of the dispute. He, pale in the face and with a tense expression, was continually silenced with every word he tried to utter. I stopped a little uncertain. I was about to approach but I feared that my presence could make things worse. Moreover, I was in a hurry to take the girl back. I ran to the villa promising to check the situation on my return.

When I entered, Imma was in the living room and doing her homework. She ran and hugged me. Bianca, with her lugubrious air, did not say a word to me and continued with her crochet hook. Irina in a corner by the fireplace, her arms folded and her expression far from cheerful, did not take her eyes away from the flame. My mother-in-law with the eternal black dress looked at me with open hostility. I turned to her resentfully: 'I have told you many times that you must not go to school to take Imma without warning me. "Her response was rather vague:" Saverio is the father, and the father has the right to be with his daughter "." Moreover, where is this father? I do not see him. "" He will come, "she replied," He will come when we are gone. Suddenly Immacolata softened, gave me a half smile and said:" There is no need to make a tragedy, sit down. "One of the service women brought me a chair and a few minutes later a cup of coffee. I was dumbfounded but I did not have the courage to react with excessive discourtesy especially in front of the little girl who cannot understand the reason for the contrasts between the mother and the grandmother. I sat down and drank coffee, while Imma continued to do her homework.

When we went out, evening was falling; there was no sign of Stefano and the three thugs. On the way back, I stopped in front of the main entrance, got Imma up to Angela and went to the supermarket to do some shopping. I did not waste much time, I had to buy bread, milk and something else. Coming back, I thought I saw Gino with others in a stationary car, but it was a fleeting feeling, it was dark and I thought I was wrong. I parked the car in the back, as usual, and went upstairs to Angela. I stopped for a few minutes to exchange a few words with her and Anna, the seventeen-year-old daughter, but I did not tell what I had seen in the grove. Then I went home with the baby. I wanted to go up to Margherita to get news of what had seemed to me a quarrel, but it was late and I had to prepare dinner so I promised myself to do it later.

A few minutes later, the tragedy happened.

While I was in front of the stove, screams and shouts echoed throughout the building and a great confusion came from the ground floor and the stairs. Imma was very scared. "What happened?"- I asked insistently. I was alarmed but I did not move from home, I was afraid to leave her alone and I did not want to take her with me in fear that she might witness something unpleasant. When I heard the police sirens, someone knocked on the door. It was Anna, Angela's daughter, had tears in her eyes and sobbed.

"They found Stefano in the corridor of the basements with his head smashed. My heart clenched in a grip of ice, I put my hands on my head and gave a desperate cry:" Oh my ... oh my God. . The girl tried to wipe away the tears that flowed copiously over her face, trembled, and her pallor was impressive. She added, "Mom went with Margherita to the emergency room who collapsed."

The following period was terrible. Margherita was hospitalized in shock, with diabetes decompensated and in addition serious heart problems. Imma, for the trauma she suffered, spent her nights in nightmares. I was distressed by the scruples and fears of not having informed anyone of the scene seen in the park of the villa. Needless to deny that I was afraid to speak but I realized that the more time passed, the more my silence three became a serious omission.

My mind obsessively reworked what happened, I constantly analysed the times and the facts. No doubt Stefano had been killed in the park, but why? What had caused such a sentence? Didn't he pay a bribe or was there anything else I did not know about? Maybe I should have stepped that day in the grove but I didn't think the situation was so serious, and then my intervention would have served? Moreover, the presence of Gino in that car parked under the house? At that point, it was clear why he was there.

Why had I not said anything about what I had seen? My cowardice repelled me and made me feel guilty.

Margherita and Angela have replaced the family I no longer have and their problems are also mine. Margherita's suffering from Stefano's loss made me deeply sad. I have been by her side and I have tried to comfort her, even if it is not easy to find my words in situations of this type.

A few days after the event, the police called me. A marshal, an individual with an anonymous appearance and imperturbable expression, put me through a series of questions. "That day she parked the car at the back of the building and walked the corridor of the basements at the exact time when that man was killed in that very place". "Yes" I replied- "And you saw nothing? Have you not seen cars, people or maybe shadows, outside, on the open space or inside, in the corridor? Have you not heard any voices, discussions or unusual sounds?" "No, I have not seen anyone and I have not heard anything.""So you're in the same place of a murder in the same hour and you don't see anything, doesn't it seem strange to you?" "It may be strange but it is so". Fear gripped me; I felt a lump in my throat that choked me, and my voice came out hoarse and feeble. He looked at me inquisitively. "Where had she gone before?" She asked me again. "Shopping", but then I realized that it was useless to prevaricate and I continued: "I went to Marra family's villa to pick up my daughter. I don't know if she knows that I married one of the ..." He has short cut: "We know. What time did you get out of there?" "Around seven". "And then?" "Then I accompanied my daughter to the building entrance and went to the supermarket." My mind reeled in an effort to find generic, non-compromising answers. "And she came back at about seven forty-five.

When did you go up to the first floor, did you meet the victim on the stairs?" "No, but I saw Stefano in the afternoon when he went out and I went in." He continued, "The body was discovered by the tenant on the third floor around eight. Where was she?" "At home"."These are the times, the killers perhaps have lurked there somewhere, they will surely have made some noise, a thump, a crunch, footsteps, the victim will have screamed, will have said something ... and she hasn't heard anything? ""Maybe, if I had seen or heard I would have died too, if I am alive it means that I have not seen anything"-"That's the point." At that moment, I did not understand what he meant. Finally, irritated, I looked him in the eyes and said to him."Marshal, but do you know that a person can also be killed in a place other than where he is found?" He looked at me with the same impassive air and simply nodded.

In the evening, while tidying up the kitchen I reflected once again on what had happened. What I could not understand was why they had not hidden Stefano's body somewhere as they usually did. Could it be that they organized all this to involve me? I was seized with an ever-growing sense of anguish. I shuddered at the thought that Imma and I could have witnessed the murder in the grove, it would have been enough to refuse coffee and to leave the villa a few minutes earlier.

I thought about the marshal's insistent questions and carefully analysed my statements, I had the impression that I had said something wrong without understanding what.

Suddenly I understood, I realized that I had made a serious mistake. I felt in danger and I had the feeling that something was going to happen to me. Dejected, I looked at my daughter, then, I took my head in my hands in desperate search for a solution. She was doing her homework, I approached her and I caressed her, at that moment the only possible way out came to my mind. "Forget your homework," I said, "tomorrow you won't go to school. Mom will take you to another place. Now go to bed because tomorrow morning we will have to get up early." The next day I woke her up at dawn, I gathered her things in a bag, I put her on the best dress; I combed her carefully and put a blue bow in her hair. At the station, we got on the train to Naples. "Where are we going mom?" She asked me. "Then you'll see," I replied without adding anything else. Arriving in Naples, from Piazza Garibaldi, a public transport took us to our destination.

As soon as I got off the bus, I felt a dark sense of bitterness; those places made me remember many memories and many regrets. Imma looked around perplexed. At the sight of the building, I felt myself failing and a painful twinge crossed my stomach. I would have run away but I strengthened myself and went on. Luckily, the front door was open, they were doing the cleaning. I slipped inside avoiding meeting the concierge. Nothing had changed. Everything was the same. We made the stairs on foot and on the second floor; we found ourselves in front of a door. I had a boulder on my chest; I let out a deep sigh and knocked. A young woman, not very tall, with delicate features and a long, slightly wavy brown hair, appeared in the doorway, opened a small window and looked at me questioningly.

Then she saw Imma and a slight smile lit her face. He looked at me uncertain again. "I'm Elisa," I said. She replied- "I am Giulia", and opened the door wide to let me in. I stopped hesitantly and dropped a fearful glance inside the apartment. She immediately dispelled my doubts: "There is no one; I am alone in the house".

Shortly after in the kitchen, while preparing the coffee, she told me about the family. "We came to live here not to leave only your father who after his mother's death had fallen into a deep state of depression. She spoke and I observed those familiar environments and it seemed to me that I had never left. Kitchen modern furniture replaced the old ones, suitable for a young married couple; but the references were always those: the window on the park, the mahogany door, the coloured tiles. "I'm sorry I have nothing to offer the girl," she said, handing me the cup, "when I saw you I had the impression of knowing you, but I couldn't understand who you were, maybe you were in some old family photos".

I listened to her little; my thought was lost in the swarm of memories that crowded in the mind. Suddenly my attention was drawn to her speech. She told me that they had been trying to have a child for a long time, but to no avail, they had consulted many doctors but every attempt had failed. It seemed to me a favourable circumstance and then I introduced the purpose of the visit. "Maybe I will have to get away from home for a while and I can't take the girl with me, I need trusted family people to leave her, that's why I came here 'Giulia looked at Imma as if she were a treasure chest jewels, and a radiant light has appeared in her gaze. "Of course, you can leave her to me as much as you want," she replied happily. "Don't you want to ask Guido?"- I asked her. "Don't worry, he will definitely agree"

I left before my brother and father returned, with great pain in my heart. Imma's tears were unstoppable, when she understood the situation she started to cry and rattle, she clung to me screaming and she did not want to leave me anymore. She was pulling my dress, holding me tight, she did not understand why I wanted to abandon her in that unknown house; I promised her to come back soon but she did not listen to me. I was destroyed, annihilated by. Fortunately, Giulia with her sweetness managed to calm her and I realized that this was the ideal solution; my mother-in-law would never know where her granddaughter was.

A few days later, the police came to pick me up and brought me here. Murder competition is the accusation, but when the magistrate interviewed me, I realized that it is a pretext; the investigators know that I have nothing to do with the murder but they also know that I know. The autopsy showed that Stefano was not killed in the corridor of the basements but perhaps in a garden, a park, a forest or something like that because they found leaves, soil, and grass on his clothes and they understood that I knew it because it resulted from my deposition made a few days earlier. They probably guessed how things went, I was about to give up but I strengthened myself, I did not have to be weak and suggestible. On the other hand, I had imagined that that sentence would have betrayed me, so I was not surprised when the magistrate said to me- "You told the police marshal that a person can be killed in a place other than that where he is found and things went just like that. So you know how the events went ". I did not admit and I did not deny, but he relied on my feelings of guilt, on my scruples and reminded me that Stefano was a good person and was the husband of a friend. He also reminded me that code of silence helps criminals and harms justice. He would like you to tell me everything I know about Marras and he made me a proposal, I reserved the right to think about it. When they called me for the interview with the family, I was dumbfounded, I have no relatives who can come to visit me and I thought that perhaps Angela and Margherita had had some special permission. Entering the room, I saw Imma accompanied by Giulia. She had a beautiful little red and white dress with a fur hat and matching shoes, a surely expensive dress, and she clutched a teddy bear that she caressed delicately. As soon as she saw me, she ran to embrace me happy, I held her close to me, I gave my sister-in-law a look of gratitude and I cried with emotion. "I told her that you were hospitalized, she wanted to see you and it seemed right to please her", said Giulia, "Guido and dad were happy to have her at home and bought her many toys. Even if she always thinks about you, she is settling in with us, she understood that we love her. How can you not love such a sweet little girl? "

Yesterday they came again and my brother was with them, he hugged me without speaking, he was visibly excited and he told me that he contacted a good lawyer. I realize that Guido must have made a great sacrifice to come here; he would never have imagined having to enter a prison. I feel great regret at the thought that I forced my parents to have this unpleasant experience. Imma had another nice dress and always clutched the same stuffed animal. "She has grown fond of that teddy bear and always carries it with her, and she never leaves even during the night." Giulia explained to me smiling. "We have prepared a small room with coloured furniture, she liked it very much "-I have the certainty that my daughter is treated like a little princess, on the other hand how could it be otherwise? She is surrounded by the love of her closest relatives.

This was the main factor, which convinced me to accept the proposal that the police asked me.

144

I realized that so far I have moved away from evil but have not tried to fight it. Of course, heroic behaviour could not be expected from me, I did not have the opportunity to act differently, but today I have this possibility. For some time now, my husband's family is under investigation, as all those who, like satellites, go around him. My testimony would certainly be important. I was asked to tell everything I learned when I lived in that house and I will do it, whatever the cost. I will say about the murder of Luca, Dora's boyfriend, about the fire of the electrical appliance store, about Stefano's murder and about many other serious events, which, in spite of myself, I had learned about.

I will be included in a protection program, I will have to change my name, job, country and I will be forced to stay away for a long time, but I am sure it is worth it. However, Imma will stay where she is, in a family that loves her and will offer her everything I could not have given her. She will always stay away from his father and his clan.

I know that moving away I will give her a pain as great as mine is but I hope that in time she will understand. When I come back, I will tell her the story of her mother and that of Aunt Dora.

Then it will be big enough to understand that in life, sometimes, you have to make difficult but necessary choices. I am sure that my decision will be useful for not only justice, society and my knowledge but above all, for my daughter's future and many other children who live in this land like her.

S. Maria C.Vetere 2000

MARIKA

"I'm a nomad, a Bosnian Rom gypsy," she says as I look at her in amazement. She wears a cream-colored linen suit, a matching silk scarf and heeled sandals. The brown hair cut in a bob, with a thick fringe that falls on the forehead. "This is the new look of the Gypsies?" I ask her indicating her clothing. She barely smiles. «I chose a way of life different from that of my people, it was not easy but I did it. Now I would like to be considered only Italian ». Marika is slender, nice, with a beautiful intelligent face and a sweet and sincere smile that goes straight to the heart. "There are many prejudices about Gypsy, what is not understood is that they are a people with their customs and rules, rules different from those of other peoples, and for this reason they are not understood and not accepted. Some have their own code of conduct, carry out ancient work activities, do not commit crimes and live in harmony with everyone, others instead are dedicated to theft and begging, like my family. I came into the world in a nomad camp on the outskirts of Rome, in an old shabby caravan, freezing in winter and hot in summer. I was the fifth of seven brothers, born to a Bosnian family who had settled in Italy for some time. A few months after my birth, my mother put me in a box and, as she had done with the other children, she took me with her to beg. This is obviously, because a baby girl moves the strings of pity more. I always slept; she gave me small sips of beer that kept me in a state of perpetual torpor. Some Gypsy women are convinced that beer is a tonic, while in reality it is a kind of opium, turning off the brain and dulls children's mind. At the age of four, I too began to beg, they had taught me to approach especially women, those rather elderly considered more gifted with a maternal sense. But, this theory had little response. Actually, when I held out my hand, some of them caressed me and gave me something, but others ignored me and still others pushed me away with disgust. Strangely, even though I was small, I did not accept that gesture of reaching out, I felt that it did not belong to me; I did it reluctantly only because I was forced. My brothers and I lived under a cloak of oppression and the oppressor was our father. He was always an aggressive and violent man. He did not consider our family's needs. His only interest was to satisfy his desires. He did not love anyone. He had no friends and poured out all his frustrations on his wife and children. If the proceeds from our business were unsatisfactory, when we retired in the evening, it beat us up and left us without eating. I had been fasting for whole days because I didn't bring him what he wanted. To remedy something more I had devised a stratagem, I pretended to be crippled, in the hope that people would move with compassion, and then I would blindfold or pretend to limp, but I think my fictions were not credible because the situation did not improve at all. What was the use of all the money that arrived? Just to buy luxury, powerful and expensive cars or ultra-modern cell phones while we continued to make the same miserable life.

I ate very little, dressed in rags, and in winter, the cold paralyzed my body and mind. Above all, I remember my perpetually frozen feet tucked in cotton socks and stiff wooden clogs. Sometimes my older sister, Sonia, to get me warm gave me some glasses of grappa, then my head was spinning and my stomach was boiling, I felt wrapped in a strange fog that

147

made me forget everything. Every now and then, we change cities, always settling in fields located in the extreme suburbs. Some were truly horrible, with muddy and garbage-filled terrains. I endured all those inconveniences badly and a form of hostility had created in me a resentment that I poured on the whole world.

When on the street I looked at myself in some shop windows, I saw a slender and barefoot girl with a skirt with multi-coloured flowers that made me easily identified. I had the impression that everyone looked at me with contempt, then I attacked some child in the street, just not to take something away from him, I knew he had no money, but to give vent to my anger, even if then I had to flee chased by some adult or older children. Social workers from the municipality often came to the camp, they were polite and smiling people who took care of the conditions of the children and tried to convince our parents to let us attend school. My father welcomed them with suspicion, pretended not to understand what they said and sent them back with vague promises that he would never keep. I would have liked to go to school with one of those white aprons with a blue bow, study, learn to read and write, playing with other children. Unfortunately, I did not have the opportunity to express wishes, even if, now I understand it, they were more than legitimate wishes. Instead, my wishes at the time made me feel guilty, as if they were illicit ideas to be ashamed of. At the age of ten, I began to rob the apartments with my brothers and other children in the camp. We slipped everywhere, climbing the gates, fences and gutters until we reached the lower floors. We managed to sneak into the parks, courtyards, hallways of the buildings and penetrate through windows, doors, cracks. Then, once inside, we unleashed like fury in the whole apartment grabbing what we could: gold, silver, cameras, watches, lighters, but also ornaments that seemed valuable to us, or belts, shoes, bags if new. Then we silently slipped out as we entered. Usually, the mission was successful, but even if it failed and someone discovered it, there was nothing he could do because he was faced with only children. For this reason, we faced fearlessly every situation, convinced that we were protected from our childhood.

Of course, we didn't invent this technique, it was the result of long lessons given by adults. They taught us to climb quickly, to hide us cleverly, move without making noise and above all, they taught us not to be afraid because to carry out that kind of action you had to have a lot of courage. Our ability was the result of our agility. We were quick, light and much trained. I hated stealing; I did not like sneaking in, plundering, running away. I understood that it was wrong but I could not oppose it and then I followed the current that forced me to do what I didn't want. Then something happened that created a sense of rebellion in me for that life and laid the groundwork for the radical change that would take place.

We were in Bari during the summer season, me and two other children from the camp managed to enter a villa, the windows on the ground floor were open, and the shutters almost all lowered, perhaps because of the heat. It was easy enough to introduce us first into the garden and then into the house through the crack of a not completely closed shutter. A dark gloom reigned in the interior, we moved groping and with great caution, we were experts in this. We realized we were in the kitchen, everything seemed clean and tidy, a drop of water falling from the tap marked the seconds. Inexplicably, I felt a negative feeling, a strange premonition and if I had the chance, I would have fled. I lagged behind my companions. From the kitchen, we entered the corridor, which was also dark, trying to orientate ourselves to understand where to go. Suddenly the door of a room opened and on the threshold there was the outline of a huge being, a big man, a kind of giant who with all the breath he had in his body uttered an inhuman cry, grabbed the two children by the arms and threw them forcefully against the wall like two useless rags. In panic, I looked around, framed the front door and, while I heard the screams of my friends, I rushed out terrified. Without looking back, I flashed through the garden and found myself on the road. I continued to run with my heart in my throat for a long time as if I a ghost was following me, until, left out of breath, I found myself in an area of the city that I did not know at all and understood that I was lost. Exhausted I sat on the steps of a church and started to cry. I didn't know how to go back to the camp and maybe I didn't even want to go back. I feared my father's reaction to the theft failure and that of everyone else because I had fled without worrying about my companions, abandoning them in that house in the clutches of that monster. People hurried by, it was lunchtime, but nobody worried about that gypsy girl in tears on the steps of a church. I saw children more or less my age, returning from school with the backpack on their shoulders. They shook their mothers or fathers' hands, jumping happily protected by the presence of their parents. Why wasn't I like them? Why couldn't I go to school like my other peers instead of being forced to steal and beg? I had a rage and sobbed even louder, when suddenly someone noticed me and touched me. "Why are you crying?" She asked.

It was a young woman who looked at me with a worried expression; I gave her a suspicious look. "Don't worry. I don't want to hurt you, why are you crying?' She repeated." I answered I got lost. "Where do you live?" "I do not know". "Maybe you're in the nomad camp?" "I don't know," I repeated. "How old are you?" "Maybe eleven." "Poor little girl! Are you hungry? "I answered: "I'm always hungry". She took me by the hand." Come, I'll take you to me", she said. She lived with her mother in a building not far away in a beautiful bright and well-furnished house, with a big kitchen and a large terrace. I had seen so many luxurious apartments thanks to many thefts I had committed, but that struck me particularly. "In the future I will live in a house like this," I thought. It was the first time I had made plans of that type. The mother was as kind as her daughter, who was not shocked by a barefoot and dirty gypsy. She made me have a shower and then she gave me a clean shirt that fit me too big, but it was always better than the rags I had. They gave me many things to eat, for me a complete lunch from the first course to the fruit was something I had never seen. At table I spoke little, the essentials, I was afraid of saying something wrong and of losing that friendship, but they showed comprehension and affection. I believe they knew the dynamics of my environment. They asked me about my parents but when they noticed my uncertainty and fear of speaking, they did not go deeper. I knew that the young girl's name was Claudia and was a social worker, like those who came to the camp, while the mother was a teacher. "That's what the teachers are like," I thought, "affable people who treat children gently."

After lunch Claudia took me back to the camp, the happy parenthesis was over. Before leaving me, she said, "If you need help come to me, you know where to find me": I was very sad, I wanted to thank her but I did not find the words, tears came down on my face and that was my parting. As I came back home, I was thinking with apprehension about the failed theft in the villa and of my escape. I could imagine my father's anger and that of my parents' parents, who knows what would have happened to me! Instead, no one scolded me, not even my father. I knew that my friends had been at the hospital with head injury and fractures in various parts of the body. We had stumbled upon the home of a violent psychopath who was often treated in a psychiatric clinic and who had massacred them. That fact opened my mind, I understood that sneaking into other people's homes, as we did, was very risky, we could meet people of all kinds: deranged, violent, maniacs, pedophiles, and we were defenseless in the face of such people. I felt deceived, what they had always said was not true, that is, that we should not be afraid because no one could harm us. They exploited us, they had always exploited us, and taking advantage of our naivety, they sent us to the fray. Nobody cared about our safety.

I confided in my sister Sonia, she was the eldest daughter and my only sister, the rest were all male. She cooked, mended, washed, and performed the functions of mother, since our mother was an almost non-existent amorphous being. She did not take care of anything, neither of cooking nor of raising children. Her only concern consisted in avoiding irritating my father: an arduous undertaking since a trifle was enough to make him explode. I told Sonia that I was no longer going to ransack the houses. She looked at me worried. She knew that my father would not take it well. Her face was skinny, hollowed out, the skeletal body, she was twenty but she seemed forty years old. She, too, was proved by that miserable existence, but she was convinced that this was the only possible life. I knew that there were other ways of living, even for a nomad. She promised to speak to our father, but he became furious, he turned to my mother aggressively and with a stick in his hand. "This isn't my daughter, she's too rebellious," he said. She didn't say a word, she turned pale and maybe she thought her time had come. She was about to throw them at that stick, but the children stopped him and convinced him that, all in all, I could do also other things, to continue begging for example, which was a little risky activity, or to devote myself to some occasional snatch.

I had not forgotten about Claudia and every now and then, when I could, I ran to her and her mother. Seeing them, even if only for a few minutes, made me feel better. They always welcomed me with affection and gave me something to eat. No money, they never gave it to me because they knew where it was going. Therefore, I experienced how important it was to have a friend; a person who listens, advises, identifies, and understands. My father didn't like that friendship, according to his point of view it was a deviant acquaintance, there was the risk that I would become a decent girl and so he decided to change the city. I was desperate, I would have never seen Claudia and her mother again, I could not write to her because I was illiterate and I did not have a cell phone to make some calls. Suddenly, I was deprived of great emotional and moral support.

We moved to Pescara, in a field outside the city. For two years, I hadn't seen Claudia, only sometimes I could phone her from a public telephone box, as far as my shortage could allow. One day I found in my hands a rather large sum, unexpectedly obtained from alms. An idea flashed in my mind and I immediately put it into practice without thinking more than a while. Instead of returning to the camp, I went to the train station and bought a ticket to Bari. It was the first time I travelled by train and it was an unforgettable experience. I watched the travellers, listened to their speeches and tried to guess where they were going, what they thought and what their problems were. I looked at the view from the window, in front of me paraded: sea, countryside, woods, inhabited areas, and then again trees, fields and sea. Everything attracted my attention, everything seemed beautiful and interesting to me. The controller looked at me suspiciously, but said nothing, simply cancelled the ticket. From Bari station, I managed to walk to Claudia's house trusting my memories and asking whoever was able to provide them with information.

I arrived exhausted and happy. Claudia welcomed me happily but perplexed. She knew that she could not keep me with her. My father had immediately filed a disappearance report. She tried to get me into a community or a family home where I could study and escape the nomadic life, but it was not possible, and a few days later the female police brought me back to the Pescara camp. My father's anger was unspeakable, for more than a month, I had carried the signs of his beatings on my body, but I did not give up and began to plan a new escape. I didn't have time to implement it because a few months later I was arrested and taken to the juvenile prison. That day I had thought of stealing something to bring more money to my father and get his forgiveness. I caught sight of an elderly lady, who certainly had a lot of money. I tried to take her by surprise, I thought she would give up immediately and instead when I tried to steal her bag, she became a hyena and began to scream with strong

154

resistance, but then she left the grip and she fell on the ground, breaking her femur. As usual, I was naive and unwary. Instead of running away immediately, I stood there pulling my purse and watching if the old woman had hurt herself, thus giving some people time to catch me and hand me over to the police.

I had suspended sentences and, at the end, I had to serve a year's sentence. In the juvenile, after all, I didn't find myself so bad, the worst inconvenience was certainly imprisonment. For me, who was used to being out on the streets all day, being always locked in was a torture. In the early days, I felt a sense of oppression that blocked my breath. Then, I got used to it, also because they organized many activities that distracted me. For the rest, there were also positive aspects. First, the fact that we ate every day, for better or for worse, we ate from breakfast to dinner. Not to mention that some companions received food from the families they shared with the others. I was amazed to see how many operators worked in that institution. Many people committed to us, overseers, teachers, educators, social workers, doctors, nurses. A migraine, an abdominal pain, a toothache, were immediately treated.

My family didn't show up, only Sonia came to visit me twice. "How fat you are!" She said, amazed. "I eat here and I don't work, and then I do gymnastics, I play volleyball, I go to school, and I am preparing a play ..." He looked at me in astonished, poor Sonia! It seemed strange to her that there were so many activities in a prison other than working. Inside there, I met some girls, poor unfortunate more or less like me. Among them Monica, a toxic employee who had committed an infinite number of crimes to get drugs: thefts, muggings, robberies. She was the daughter of good people; her parents came to the interview every week and brought her clean food and linen; A few hours after her arrival she fell into a withdrawal crisis, suffering a lot, sweated and, at the same time, she was cold, she felt muscle contractions and stomach cramps. I was impressed. I had never seen a person in withdrawal. Here, the drug does not circulate, we do not consume it or we sell it, we are against it, even if not everyone follows this rule.

Monica and I became friends. She was very generous; she always shared what she had with everyone. She was also educated but, recently, because of the drug, she dropped out of school. We spent a long time together and did the same things. Her problem was addiction; she could not help staying without heroin. "Mine is a psychological addiction and it is worse than physical addiction," she said. One day she told me that he wanted to escape and she asked me to go away with her. "What is it for? After a while they come to pick you up and bring you back inside with the penalty supplement," I replied. "I'm not going home," he said. "And where do you go?" "Where it happens, I don't know yet," She fled alone. Early one morning, with the complicity of a companion, she broke into the kitchens, hid in the courtyard and got into the garbage truck as it was about to leave. It was a no-brainer, which cost her dearly. When they noticed her absence, the alarm rang and we were all locked up inside our cells. Investigations began. They looked for her at her house, questioned her parents, but the poor people knew nothing, they questioned me too, but I was a grave. They looked for her a little everywhere, at friends and relatives' home, but especially in places hanged out with drug addicts. After two days, they found her in the bathroom of a slum. She had died from an overdose. It was a shock for all. No one could have imagined such a tragic end. My pain was great. I spent many days in tears crying even for those poor parents.

In the juvenile, I finally had the opportunity to study and learn to read and write, and it was a great result for me. I could read the names of the streets, the billboards, the city bus boards and, of course, books, and then I could write. As soon as I could, I sent a letter to Claudia, it was short and rather elementary but it was a letter. She immediately replied and praised me for this achievement. At that time I definitely got the idea that I was not made for nomadism, I wanted a real job, a husband who would not mistreat me and a normal family. When I left the prison, I went back to the camp and found everything as I had left it: the old caravan, the misery, the cold, the discomforts, the apathy of my mother, the irascibility of my father. However, I had changed my mind style and I couldn't stand this anymore. I said that I had learned to read and that I was one of the few educated in the midst of a pack of illiterate people, I thought I aroused esteem and admiration among them, but the news was received with the utmost indifference. What was the use of reading? Maybe it got you something to eat? No. Therefore, everyone concluded that it was no use.

By now I was seventeen and I had become a woman, many at the camp looked at me with interest. One evening Sonia revealed to me: "Dad found you a husband." "A husband? I'm not going to marry a Gypsy to move from one boss to another," I said. She objected that the suitor was rich, had a luxurious Mercedes and many horses, but I didn't know what to do with the Mercedes and the horses. When they made me meet him, I was shocked, he was horrible, short, thin as a nail, completely bald and with few teeth in the mouth, it was not even clear how old he was. Needless to externalize my dissent in the family, it was better to carry out another escape, and so did I. The next day I ran to the station and got on any train, without even knowing where it was going.

Unfortunately the inspector spotted me immediately, asked me for the ticket and the documents. Since I had neither, he handed me over to the railway police. They took me back to the camp and I had to suffer my father's anger for the umpteenth time, I was used to it by now. From that modest escape, however, there was a positive result: my fiancé dissolved his promise. He was not going to marry a woman who refused him. There were many young people in this world. He would surely have found another available. That man showed more brain than anyone did. Since then my father tried to get me married countless times, always with unlikely people. There was only one young man I liked, but that engagement lasted three days because he was killed in a firefight in mysterious circumstances that nobody ever wanted me to clarify.

I understood that I had to wait for the age of majority to get rid of that life and my father. Surely, he would pretend to exploit me forever, but, once I was of age, he could no longer turn to the police to get me back. The day of my eighteenth birthday was completely ignored, no party, no cake, no greetings as other Earthlings do. Sonia gave me a comb; otherwise, nobody attached importance to the anniversary, while I exulted inside myself. I was finally able to implement my escape plan. I had saved a small sum and had hidden it in a place that had seemed safe. Unfortunately one of my brothers had found it and I was left without money. Certainly, the lack of money would not have prevented me from running away.

One morning I left the house rather early and went to the ATM. I was trying to find a suitable subject for my purpose. She had to be a woman, not too young, because she would have had the strength to react, nor too old, because she could have created problems. After a long wait, the right person finally arrived; she was a short-sighted and somewhat clumsy lady.

I waited for her to pick up and put away the money, then, I went out of the hiding place and gave her a push making her fall down. Without giving her time to realize what was happening, I stole her purse and ran away. I ran like a crazy for a long time until I was out of breath. When I arrived in an area far from snatching, I checked the amount of the loot and I saw that it was a substantial amount. I went to a local market that was nearby and, on a second-hand stand, I bought an ordinary but nice dress and a pair of high-heeled shoes for little money. I sneaked into the toilet of a crowded bar and changed quickly. I finally got rid of those hateful Gypsy clothes. That snatch was the last illegal act of my existence. I swore that from that moment on everything would change. At the station, I saw on the board that the first leaving train was for Naples and then I made the ticket. I had never been to that city. I found it very chaotic. The square in front of the station was invaded by a flood of cars, public vehicles and pedestrians. It looked like an interlocking game, a kind of puzzle where all the pieces gradually found their place. I had a moment of dismay, I didn't know where to go and I wandered the streets aimlessly. I had to look for accommodation before it got dark and then a job that would allow me to survive. I got an idea, I knew that priests help people in difficulty; they had done it with me in the past too, so I came in a church. I found a young priest full of good intentions, Don Pino. He said that for the first few times I could eat at the soup kitchen and showed me an association, which dealt with foreigners in Italy. "It is not easy for you to find a job, there are many prejudices about Gypsy", he said. The association was made up of volunteers and community workers and was mainly interested in black people. I found a place with some non-EU citizens in old and dilapidated rooms located in the old part of the city. For me, that temporary condition was no worse than the caravan and nomad camps, where I had lived all my life. I adapted easily. I was also offered occasional jobs in the countryside or at the fruit and vegetable market, but I wanted something more stable and lasting. For many days, I searched in shops, hairdressers, clubs, restaurants, supermarkets, but without result. I was walking in a crowded street with my head in turmoil thinking about my situation when a smell of pizza caught my attention. I found myself in front of a hot rotisserie-table. A boy in the doorway was arranging sandwiches for the arancini (fried rice balls- a typical Sicilian recipe) in an external shop window. He turned to me and looked at me carefully. "Are you hungry?" He asked. I nodded. His face had an expression of solidarity mixed with compassion and he handed me a stuffed sandwich. I devoured it in a flash. "Damn what an appetite! ' he exclaimed laughing, I realized he was speaking with a foreign accent and I looked at him carefully He was a handsome young man with dark skin, raven hair and coal-black eyes.

I asked, "Aren't you Italian? No, I'm from Bangladesh. Bangladesh? Where is it?" "Asia ... India ... do you know?" "So far away?' I said amazed. He made a gesture of resignation then replied: "You are not

Italian, are you?" "I am Italian but I am gypsy" What do you mean? ""
Forget it, I'll explain you later. He had a radiant smile that highlighted his
perfect and very white teeth. "What's your name?" "Marika, what about
you?" "Rami" "Rami? What kind of name is Rami?" "And what name is
Marika?" We burst out laughing together and for a moment, I forgot my
problems. But, they immediately came back to me. "Do you know anyone
who can offer me a job?" "Here they are looking for an attendant to do the
cleaning, but the work is heavy, in the kitchen it is hellishly hot and the
pay is low. All those who occupy that place go away immediately. The last
one quit yesterday" Despite the daunting prospects my heart opened. "I
want to try," I said. Rami introduced me to the owner of the diner, a
grumpy-looking old man who looked at me skeptically, but perhaps he had
no other choice and hired me for a trial period of three days.

He immediately supplied me with a mop, rag and detergent. I had no
idea how to clean a kitchen. I had no experience with it. I took courage. "It
won't need a diploma for this," I thought. Fortunately, I was now able to
read, so I carefully studied the instructions written on the detergent bottles
and went to work. It was a great effort, it never stopped, the place was
always full and effectively in the kitchen, the heat was overwhelming. The
cook was a good man with many children to feed. He cooked with a
handkerchief around his neck that he used to dry the sweat that fell
copiously on his face. He was very fatherly. I would have had a father like
him. He had taken me in sympathy and encouraged me. "You are full of
good will, you will see that you will settle down," he said. On the third
day, the owner seemed more convinced, extended the trial period for a
week and gave me a little advance. Sometime later he put me on a white

coat, put me to serve at the counter and to withdraw the trays from the tables. I was proud to have managed to earn my living by working honestly. In the meantime, I had rented a small, modest but dignified apartment with two Moroccan girls. I started to have some hope for the future. Rami had become an important reference, it was enough for me to have him close and see his smile to feel reassured. A strong and important feeling was born between us. Every evening, even if we ended very late, he accompanied me home. We walked together on the half-deserted streets holding hands and telling each other about us. He spoke a lot. I liked listening to his warm voice and his captivating exotic accent. His is a story of poverty like that of many others who come to the West to seek fortune. A family engaged in the cultivation of rice for little money, a land tormented by cyclones and monsoons, a sick mother who does not have the opportunity to heal herself. We planned to get married and live together as soon as our finances allowed it.

Over time, he had been hired in a good restaurant with a decent wage and I had won the confidence of the owner of the cafeteria who employed me at the checkout. Almost two years had passed since I had left the nomad camp. One morning while I was on the usual streets, I heard someone calling me. It was Leda, a girl of my group. She threw her arms around my neck and kissed me affectionately. I was surprised to see her. "Where are you going?" She asked. "I go to work at the diner here on the corner and what do you do?" "What do you want me to do? I am looking for charity and I guess the future to whom wants to know it "" How come you are in Naples?" "We camped in Agnano (a city near Naples)". The news left me indifferent, by now I had almost completely forgotten my people and I had left the past behind. I didn't imagine how bad that meeting was. The next day my father sank into the rotisserie like an obsessed man, as soon as he saw me, shouting threats and insults. He grabbed me by the arm and tried to take me away. He still hadn't resigned himself to the idea of losing me. I shouted, I resisted but he was much stronger than I was. He held me tight and tried to drag me out of the club. Everyone watched the scene stunned without understanding or having the courage to intervene. Desperate, I gave him a bite in the arm with all the strength I had, slightly released his grip and I managed to get free.

I found refuge in the kitchen. He joined me and, continuing to scream, punched me in the face, lost my balance and fell to the ground. I was out of breath and my nose was bleeding profusely. The cook tried to stop him but he thrown him away like a twig. To get up I leaned on a shelf, reached out to support myself and touched a large knife. I grabbed it by the handle and as he pounced on me, I stuck it in his chest. He turned pale, looked at himself in amazement at the wound from which a copious spurt of blood was spurting out his shirt, brought a hand to his chest and passed out.

I was arrested almost immediately. I was told that my father was hospitalized and immediately underwent surgery, but he is not life threatening. Don Pino got me a lawyer, a good young man who goes to his parish and who hasn't asked about money. He said it was self-defense and I should be out soon ... Rami came to visit me, I have no doubts about him, I know that nothing can separate us.

Claudia called me. I had never lost touch with her. Now she is married. She has two beautiful girls and has remained the same good and kind person since then.

In Naples, what happened caused a sensation, newspapers and some local television spoke about it.I thought I had lost my job and instead the owner of the rotisserie wrote me that the clientele has increased. Many people go to see the place where the crime happened and therefore when I go out I will return to my place, in short, I have become an attraction. How strange people are, aren't they? I am twenty years old and I seem to be forty. Mine has been a long and difficult life experience. I stole, I suffered, I struggled, I tried to get out of a condition that kept me trapped and when I thought I was out of it now I did something I never imagined, I risked killing my father. I know that when I go out I will find Rami and other people who love me as well, but I don't think I will be able to forget all this. It is true that the past remains attached to you, it is like the shadow, it walks by your side, in front, behind you, but it will never leave you ».
Arienzo 2000

SOFIA LOREN

The following story is very different from the previous ones, since it is not marked by human or tragic aspects, which had characterized the others. However, it is to be told, because Sofia Loren's detention was a special event. The emphasis of media was so big that it cannot be ignored.

She did not give me any confidence, and, after all, I could not speak about, for privacy. She used to speak very little, maybe for prudence. Surely, it was not easy for her to face with that situation, considering her imagine safeguarding and the particular context in which it had happened. The facts represented multi-coloured spots, which joyfully had painted the grey atmosphere typical of prisons and just of these spots, I am going to tell about.

"From the Ministry, they asked for you." The operator told me at phone. "I'll convey the communication".

After a little while, an impersonal voice told me: "Am I speaking with the Director?" "Yes, I am", I answered. "I have to send you an urgent and reserved telegram". I took a sheet from the ream laying on the desk and I started to write, while the other was dictating.

"From Ministry of Justice –

General Direction of Prevention and Penalty Institute-

From Prison Department to Female Prison of Caserta.

Personally to the Director.

We communicate that today, Mrs Scicolone Sofia, called Loren, will turn herself to this Penalty Institute, born in Rome 20th September 1934 and living in Switzerland. She has to expiate one month of detention. After the registration of this communicate, your Direction will execute all the procedures, it will act using the right preventative measures, in order to guarantee the safeguard of the person; the right caution for order and security inside the institute will be set, avoiding any kind of inconvenience.

Looking forward to hearing from you.

Signature: Director of Prisoner Department."

It was known that Mrs Sofia Loren had been condemned some years before for tax evasion, caused by an irregular individual income tax return. The national press had debated the question for long and she had been far from Italy for long time, just to avoid the arrest. I read again the text of the official communication and I was thinking about what mysterious reasons had pushed the General Direction to send such a special prisoner right to the Jail in Caserta. Only after long time, I could know our prison was considered a calm institute, far from the clamour of Rome. It would not be, of course, that place to discourage photo reporters and journalists of the whole world. Just like two Japanese, who I would meet every day in front of the hall with a strange device in their hand, maybe a cam, and a printed smile on their face: "Good MoLning, Madam!" They said with a bow. In that period, Mrs Loren was one of the most famous actress in the world. She had received an Oscar reward for her role inside De Sica's film "La Ciociara". She had acted in several other movies in Italy and USA, where she is still considered a big star of sixties. Such a prominent celebrity would surely have attracted the attention of prisoners. It was inevitable that a licit curiosity would involve everyone and that curiosity would also create problems or dangers (threats, extortions, insane sexual appetite, etc.)

I went over the gate, which divided the offices from the area of detention and I reached the second floor department. I chose a cell, empty at that moment, regular in size and far from the others. The room had the same furniture: a bed, an iron night table, single little red- rust coloured Formica wardrobes. No difference nor for what concerned the structure: white walls, grey marbled floor, glazed ceramics toilets and white majolica coverings.

That cell will be going to represent the target of many curiosities. Many people wondered which particular features would it have and what sort of luxury would be there inside, to become the cell of a star of that size. Therefore, it had been difficult to believe that was a simple cell of few squared metres, with standard furniture and a little TV, nothing else.

The news of that event travelled at a supersonic speed and few hours later, it had been spread all over Italy. TV news broadcasted her arrival at the airport of Ciampino, near Rome. From there, she went to the Police station, complaining to expiate a penalty due to the incompetence of an accountant, died too soon, responsible of a faulty individual income tax return. I saw her on TV screen, besieged by a crowd of Journalists who were collecting her complaining, followed by cams, microphones, which popped out from everywhere.

At the time of the arrival, all the staff, usually wanting, was all complete there, even that officers who had just finished their shift, even those in day off. Everyone was there, nervously awaiting the big event. Bigger was Prisoners' turmoil, acknowledged by TV RAI channel about the great guest's arrival. Having Sofia Loren as a prisoner fellow was a sensational prospective and even inconceivable.

She arrived escorted by three police cars, from which handsome young chiefs and vice-chiefs and several officers came out. They had to fight to get her safe over the barrier made of journalists, cameramen, photo reporters, curious people collected in the little square in front of the Institute. The crowd was so big that three officers could almost and with difficulty close the front door behind her, avoiding the hall was invaded by the shouting crowd.

As soon as she came in, she appeared frightened and confused. Her emotion was big, of course. The emotional impact was undoubtedly traumatic. The fast passage from the exiting crowd outdoor and the cold reality of the prison indoor caused her a sudden pale on her face and a spontaneous silence for few minutes. Her lawyer spoke for her: He made greetings, kindly towards everyone of us. He thanked the escort and exchanged some words of circumstance with the chief of Police. He took information dealt with the organization of the institute, taking notes of timetables and days for the visits. He tried to reassure her, asking for her news. After having underlined us some obvious things, he went away.

She remained there, alone, looking around disoriented, without knowing well what to do or what to say. There was no more the impetuous "pizzaiola" who had conquered the heart of Italians from cinema's screens. There was simply only a woman, astonished and misplaced for the loss of a primary gift: freedom.

I was impressed by her thinness and height, emphasized by her very high heels, which let her overlook the others for at least few inches. She dressed in a simple bice-green suit, by Valentino, which gave her an elegant and sober appearance. It was possible to notice her own proud personality, but her style was not natural. It had to be the result of many studies and trainees. Moreover, she showed a haughty and royal behaviour, got mild by the realistic need of the moment to get down from her throne. It was clear that she was forced to be kind with everyone, hiding the need to be alone. She spoke very little; she did not give comments or make requests, no complaints. That would have been her behaviour during all the period of detention. She knew that privileged people are not allowed to complain about something wrong with her own. In the office, she gave us her personal details, her money, her jewels: a big, rigid decorated bracelet, an elegant ring of diamonds, and a flashy locket of fine manufacturing, clearly precious. -"Don't worry." She said, while the jewels were placed carefully inside a safe. -"Everything is false. Today nobody wears golden objects."

This was a notoriety period for our prison and our staff. We all had been overwhelmed by media assaults, unbelievable for whom works and lives in the dark reality of prisons. We were on a big stage, continually named, judged, questioned by means of communications of the country. Most of local citizens and some special persons in Caserta pretended to see, meet, and take pics with my permission. We were on newspapers, magazines, in interviews never done or manipulated. Pictures conveniently taken out of focus or photo montages with the spot: "Sofia Loren behind the metal grill of her cell in the prison of Caserta", or "Mrs Loren in her cell while she is eating her lunch made by a restaurant".

The interest went over the national borders, spreading out Europe and USA. Newspapers like Washington Post, New York Times, and Chicago Tribune tried several phone contacts, with a lot difficulty because of the language. (At that time, only few people could speak English) "Do you speak English?" It was the inevitable question. "No, I don't", it was the persistent answer. At that point, we could hear some Italo-American person of second or third generation, maybe picked up in that moment inside the redaction office, who, in a strange idiom of Calabro-Pugliese mixed dialect language, tried to establish an incomprehensible dialogue: What is she eating?- Che stà a magnà? What is she saying? - Che dice? Is there a swimming pool inside? –Che ce stà a piscin là? Even the European press tried to call us, with uncertain fortune. Language was a big obstacle. Besides, I remember to have spoken with a magazine director of Munich who by a good Italian, made a lovable conversation, at the end of which, he asked the spelling of my surname, in a typical German style. Italians were not different: sometime bashfully, other arrogantly, they tried to be acknowledged about everything, and when the news were not enough they used original and funny tricks. Someone called imitating the voice of Alberto Sordi or Walter Chiari. Others, pretending to be Carlo Ponti or Federico Fellini's secretary.

Rita Dalla Chiesa was very young at that time. She introduced herself as a Copy-editor of a magazine. She had a preferential path. I had received her at home for an interview. She was The General of Armed Forces Carlo Dalla Chiesa's daughter, who I had met personally, because he had studied the security question inside the prison. In that period, he was the City Prefect in Palermo and after few month, he would have been murdered by mafia killers together with his wife. Rita was young, joyful, kind with a great communicability. She was interested in the human aspect of the event and she focused on Sofia's marriage, which, just in that period was

170

uncertain. She was critical towards Carlo Ponti, who had not showed enough love to his wife Sofia. "He should have given her flowers, at least". She said, ignoring that the cell of a prison is not just like the room of a luxurious hotel.

A crowd of journalists and curious people was standing in front of the institute even at night, waiting for who knows what. "Why this prison? Why this Prison is so special to host such a big star? What is she saying? What is she writing? What does she eat? The last question was a real earworm. -"Why does everyone ask that question?" I asked to a reporter, coming from Rome. - "I don't know, everyone wants to know it and I ask for it, me too. Maybe the readers are interested." I asked it to the Nun inside the prison. "What does she eat?" "Don't you see how she is slim? What do you think she can eat? Yesterday she ate a solid egg, salad and fruits". Then, I asked again the same question to Sofia. "Why everyone asks me what do you eat?" "Because people think a star can't help eating lobsters, caviar and other sophisticated food." she said ironically. "Just for this reason, they have written about the restaurant meals. They do not think I could feel satisfied by what government passes by. Food is people's status symbol index, what distinguishes rich from common people. Other times! Today, the modern status symbol is starving."

She used to spend her days closed in her cell, reading newspaper or magazines, watching TV, writing and answering to hundreds of letters she received daily. She used to wear jeans and simply shirt but she had never forgot her high heels and her long false eyelashes. "I have taken this decision to come back to my country and to visit my mother, who is old and she cannot travel easily. I am worried about my children: I don't want that their friends at school could tell them their mother is into jail". She was worried about her family. She had also written to our President of Republic Sandro Pertini to get Clemency. Surely, her lawyers had assured her about it. However, the President did not give her the Clemency. He argued that he had been in prison too, the hardest one, the prison of past time, without any guarantees and comforts. "So, Mrs Loren will be there, where she is now. I am inflexible."

Maria Scicolone (Sofia's sister) told me that Mrs Loren was a victim of a series of misunderstanding, caused by carelessness, omissions, neglects and maybe even her own superficialities, because of her concentration on career. "What I can't stand is the irony on this event", she said. "People are making a drama of only one month of jail. I think Irony should be used for Italy, a strange country, which cannot find the right measure of things. How was it possible not to avoid all that comedy by a simple penalty fee?" Father Antonio Lisondrini, a Franciscan priest, old friend and confident of the couple Ponti- Loren, came and visited her. "I am afraid of the sadistic morbidity I can see in that greedy searching of news. I can feel a thin pleasure in perceiving Loren's misfortune by most of people. She is now the fallowing down star, of whom nobody would miss the last show. It is true: "Life is Vanity".

She used to speak very little: I do not know if she was naturally speechless or she was confused about the whole situation. She tried to show her off as less as possible, as she would confuse herself with the walls of the cells, hoping to be ignored, but she could not. She was too cumbersome.

The other prisoners had waited a couple of days that she was at easy, just because they pretended soon to be taken into consideration. Why did she behave in that way? Why was she staying closed among four walls, without giving any attention to others? She was a woman like the others, so she had to displace herself without any excuse.

She accepted to meet them during the break. She met them in the courtyard where she spoke and answered about her life: from her private to her professional one. She had all type of requests: advice or recommendations, for a probably artistic life or a guarantee for a bank loom, gossip on celebrities, the prize of her clothes or jewels. I remember that meeting in a bright day of June. All of them dressed with their best clothes, they put their make up on, as for a party and they had received her clapping and giving flowers. Some of them, who came from Africa, made a sort of show with ethnic dance and music. A gipsy woman gave her little baby into her arms. "When I get out I come and visit you, so you can give me a present", she said with her decayed smile. "I will come and see you, me too. I need a good job. I can be your personal housekeeping, tiding your cloths and your things", another said. "I need to work", she added, "I am here by mistake, they had accused me to have made a robbery in a jewellery, but it not true. It was a misunderstanding." Many of them had received gifts such as a little radio, a cassette player, a silk skirt, a styled scarf, sunglasses, a belt and something else.

In the meanwhile, the press was writing the oddest news: as for example, every day she had meals at a close restaurant, or every night she met Carlo Ponti, or famous film directors were secretly going to set a new movie inside the jail. Odd things impossible to realize. An exclusive treatment was obligated. "I am totally available for you" the Director said, "come and sit, do you like your cell? Do you want a stair carpet? You can have everything you want!

A public Prosecutor in Santa Maria Capua Vetere (a little city near Caserta) came to the jail for an inspection. He had known from newspaper that Mrs Loren had been receiving privileges. He looked around with suspicion, carefully observing the structure, which he had already known, visiting the areas for common activities and he pretended to be brought into the section. There he got near Mrs Loren's cell and he saw her through the gate while she was reading. "Who are you?" he asked with severe voice. "Nobody" she answered. "Well, well." he said satisfied. He went away soon. "I haven't noticed any privileges, the cell is like the others, she is closed inside, but I hope there won't be any preference", he said worried. That question: "Who are you?" and that answer "Nobody", made us laughing for long. The fact became an anecdote to be told to friends and relatives and make them laugh, too. "The Public Prosecutor is not updated" the staff said ironically. "He does not read newspapers, nor watch TV or go to the Cinema. He has never seen La Ciociara". When Mrs Loren had known the fact, she had a crisis of identity.

A part from hundreds of letters, she had received all type of gifts: books, pictures, drawings, photos, handmade doily, and towels. I remember a huge bouquet of one thousands of red roses with very long stems, received by an anonymous fun. The bulky gift had invaded every corner of the institute for long time. I could see those red roses displaced everywhere: inside the chapel, infirmary, cells, offices, along the hallways, they were also put at offices' home or on the tombs of their dead relatives and even at theirs children school, as a gift for their teachers. Who could spend such a fortune? Maybe Carlo Ponti or Marcello Mastroianni?

People were talking a lot about Mastroianni, (a famous Italian actor of 60s, often in couple with Sofia in many films.) Someone said he had often come and visited Sofia inside the jail and he daily called her. It was false. He called her only once. I felt a little emotion when I recognized his voice, many times heard at cinema." I would like Sofia Knows I am near her", he said. "It is a bad moment, but it will pass as everything passes in our life, good or bad things, I would be happy to do something for her, but I don't know what to do. I will write her". I do not know if he did it.

Surely, the invasion of one thousand of red roses is not a big event, even if it is unique, but there were other facts not so irrelevant, showing how much harmful could be a morbid curiosity. The jail was a very old building, adapted as a penalty institute in the first half of 19th Century. Therefore, there was not the walking area and places for sentry boxes. That lack was the origin of many problems. A photographer reached the roof climbing on the back, using a chord stairs. The area where he went did not look on the prison but I did not know that. By one hand, he kept the cam and with the other, he kept hardly himself to the drainpipe. The height was considerable and the dangerous stunt would risk to become a tragedy, even for his insistence. he did not want to give up away his feat. -"How did you get the top?"- The chief of police asked him. -"I don't know,"- He answered. -"But now I am here and I will stay there until I get a Loren's photo behind the gate, even if this means waiting for the whole month". – "Now we will let you get down."- The chief replied patiently. "Forget it! I will never move"- "If you insist we will arrest you, you know that". The threat was successful, but only after many hours and the intervention of firemen, who helped him to get down.

The morbid curiosity, however, did not attract only reporters, but also fanatics, braggers and jesters.

-"Mr Di Stefano want to speak with you."- said the officers at the gatehouse, giving me a business card: Mr Gaetano Di Stefano- Film maker. No address, no telephone number. I had never heard about him, but I did not have experience in that field.

He was an odd person, well dressed, about forty. He seemed to be in a hurry, a frantic man. "I have an urgent need to speak with Mrs Loren"- he said looking at his watch- "we should clarify some details regarding a film we will make as soon as she gets out. I am sorry: I am in a hurry. I have got a fly to Paris within two hours and I am in late"- "I am afraid but it is impossible"- I answered- "Prisoners are not allowed to talk to strangers." He showed impatience, looking again at his watch; he fidgeted in his seat with a dismay. "My God! What a disaster! How can I do now? It will be difficult to start a film within the fixed date"- he said desperate. – "could you make an exception?"- "No, I am sorry"- And I added with perplexity. - "I thought all Loren's films were made by her husband Carlo Ponti"- "Not at all!"- He strongly replied. "This film is very important. It will be set in Sicily and the cast is made up of real stars: Alberto Sordi, Giancarlo Giannini, Vittorio Gassman and the special appearance of Gina Lollobrigida (T.N= they are all famous Italian actors of 50s and 60s. Gina Lollobrigida in particular was Sophia's rival on the movie set; they had always hated each other). –"Gina Lollobrigida and Sofia Loren together?" – I said astonished- "That is impossible!"- He flashed me with angry. How did I dare him? After other precious information he gave me, although not requested, he went away in a big hurry, surely directed to Paris, always looking at his watch. When I showed his business card to Mrs Loren, she said surprized: "Who is he?"- "What? Don't you know him? He told me he has to make a film with you as protagonist, with the special guest of Gina Lollobrigida"- But it was clear at that point that I had been a victim of bragger. However, she had stopped listening to me. She was absorbed in her thoughts, she was elsewhere, as it often happened when someone told her these odd facts. Surely, she considered the effect of that big advertisement operation, created, produced and financed by the Italian Government.

Mr Di Stefano was not the only odd person who I had the chance to meet during those days. There was another strange man, who used to go up, down and around outside. When the front door was open, he mixed himself to the rest of the crowd of curious and tried to come in, asking for Loren's news or asking for meeting her, stating he was a relative. However, when we asked him the type of relative, he became elusive. "He is my fun, I think he is falling in love with me, he has always followed me since I was a girl, and I have always found him everywhere in my life. He knows all my residences, my movements, he moves together with me, wherever I go, even in USA."

There were also many supporting messages, which were appreciated, but there were also many other not acceptable. She asked to speak with me, came into my office, looking at me from the top of her two metres of height, together with her high heels and she gave me a sheet. A dense and tiny handwriting filled four pages, with a long series of insults, anathemas, contumelies. "Your sins will overwhelm you and you will be condemned for the eternity. The penalty you expiate will be never enough dreadful...God will let you fall down to hell and you will be there were you will burn among the damned shouting and screeching of teeth". Since the whole text was the same, few lines had been enough to understand and I gave her the letter back. "You should be used at this kind of things"- I said- "They are mythomaniacs or fanatics."- "No, don't stop reading, please. Read on until the end"- After a long and never ending list of dark, gloomy prophecies and predictions, at the end, the unknown writer stated this threat: "Next Friday that damned place where you are, will blow up, the earth will swallow you and you will die together with all around you, so that nobody will speak about you anymore. Signed: the Avenger!" Of course, those words came out from a crazy mind, but the thing should no more to be avoided or taken with superficiality, since it was a real dangerous threat. I told her not to say a word about the letter, because prisoners could be frightened and go in panic. However, in spite of the secret, the fact was soon spread, with the consequence of a state of anxiety felt by all of us.

The predicted explosion could be caused by a bomb, even if it was not clearly said inside the letter. Introducing a bomb into a jail was not easy. Who could make it? Prisoners' relatives, who came in, were all searched. Other hypothesis were improbable: as for example, the staff or employees who normally have free access to the offices. Maybe on the outdoor perimeter someone could easily put something. Therefore, we called the Police to ask for outside surveillance reinforces. The days after we searched all the areas, corners and the outdoor places around, but nothing similar to a bomb was found. At midnight of Friday, we were all relaxed: the dark prophecy had been a joke or the avenger had postponed his plan! It was with this doubt that after two days we had to face with another trick.

From the post office we received a huge box, addressed, guess what, to Mrs Loren, without any detail of the addressee. A stripped black and grey paper enveloped it, with a big black bow on the top. We had to search, before giving it to Mrs Loren! The size rose perplexity and suspicion, discouraging any type of approach. No one dared touch it. Many were thinking of it as a way to introduce a bomb inside the institute, even if it was not Friday. I put my ear close to the box. "If it is a bomb it is not a timing one." I said joking, but nobody appreciated it. The fact revealed all the inner worrying who nobody had never showed after the maniac's threat. When at the end, despite of fear, we opened the box, other boxes came out, one inside other, as a matrioska doll. The last one, the smallest, contained a little bear stuffed toy, which moved its hands for two minutes if you turn on a chord on the back. It was a toy. To say the truth, these jokers had taken the funny side of the event. That penalty had lost the tragic meaning of expiation, turning itself into an ironical comedy with odd text.

After few days, Mrs Loren went away at 7 o'clock in the morning to avoid the outdoor chaos of reporters, who, besides were there punctual ready to interview her, knowing fact before they happened. She dressed in an elegant white suite, by Valentino or Biagiotti, with a golden belt.

Greeting me, she left a grateful and regardful letter. "Dear Director, I wish all the unhappy prisoners, who are obliged to stay in prison could find a civil environment, respectful of basic human rights, as you have established here. Inside the heart of whom has to expiate the penalty, even if it is heavy, there is always a spark, which can light a flame of redemption. I had spoken a lot with you, observing and admiring how much wise and determination is in your soul. I thank you, my dear, for the person you are. The circumstance of our meeting has been very sad for me, but at the same time our meeting represents one of my most positive and beautiful aspect I will remember of that experience. Let me hug and thank you again. Your Sofia."

She could feel now satisfied. She had paid her debt with justice, with a great return in advertising and she could stay in her country to make a film with Lina Wertmuller, so much advertised, which besides, she had done no more.

We fell again in our anonymous world. No more interviews, no photomontages, anonymous letters, or fake bombs. So Italian people forgot earthquakes, kidnappings to deal with, to focus on the contrary, Sophia's fiscal and judiciary disadventures.

While the President Pertini let us know there would be no discount for the movie star, the spleen fell dawn on many other facts of that period. Nobody was interested in Caltagirone brothers' knots, in facts regarding Cutolo-Cirillo, the Eni-Petronim scandal, Aldo Moro's trial and other several Italian mysteries. What was important in that period were those seventeen days of prison she had to do, because of a false individual income tax and it was right she had to pay the penalty.

It does not matter if many other people, maybe less popular or less beautiful, but as rich as her, had always and methodically defrauded the Revenue, without paying nothing, stealing Italy of thousands of Billions.

Caserta 1982.

Indice

Youcanprint

Finito di stampare nel mese di luglio 2020

www.ingramcontent.com/pod-product-compliance
Lightning Source LLC
Chambersburg PA
CBHW060507290526
45791CB00001B/301